THE TUNNEL

Other Books by Russell Edson

The Very Thing That Happens
(New Directions, 1964)

What A Man Can See
(The Jargon Society, 1969)

The Childhood of an Equestrian
(Harper & Row, 1973)

The Clam Theater
(Wesleyan U. Press, 1973)

The Falling Sickness (Four Plays)
(New Directions, 1975)

The Intuitive Journey and Other Works
(Harper & Row, 1976)

The Reason Why the Closet-Man Is Never Sad
(Wesleyan U. Press, 1977)

With Sincerest Regrets
(Burning Deck, 1980)

Gulping's Recital (a novel)
(Guignol Books, 1984)

The Wounded Breakfast
(Wesleyan U. Press, 1985)

Tick Tock
(Coffee House Press, 1992)

The Song of Percival Peacock (a novel)
(Coffee House Press, 1992)

THE TUNNEL:

selected poems

Russell edson

FIELD POETRY SERIES
OBERLIN COLLEGE PRESS

The poems in this volume previously appeared in the following collections: *The Very Thing That Happens* © 1964; *What a Man Can See* © 1969; *The Clam Theater* © 1973; *The Childhood of an Equestrian* © 1973; *The Intuitive Journey* © 1976; *The Reason Why the Closet-Man Is Never Sad* © 1977; *The Wounded Breakfast* © 1985.

Publication of this book was made possible by a grant from the National Endowment for the Arts.

Library of Congress Cataloging-in-Publication Data

Edson, Russell, 1935-
    The Tunnel: Selected Poems / Russell Edson.
    (FIELD Poetry Series; 3)
    I. Title

    L.C. 93-087296
    ISBN 0-932440-66-5
        0-932440-65-7 (pbk.)

For FRANCES

CONTENTS

III From *The Clam Theater* (1973)

VII From *The Wounded Breakfast* (1985)

I

from
The Very Thing That Happens

1964

Clouds

A husband and wife climbed to the roof of their house, and each at the extremes of the ridge stood facing the other the while that the clouds took to form and reform.

The husband said, shall we do backward dives, and into windows floating come kissing in a central room?

I am standing on the bottom of an overturned boat, said the wife.

The husband said, shall I somersault along the ridge of the roof and up your legs and through your dress out of the neck of your dress to kiss you?

I am a roof statue on a temple in an archaeologist's dream, said the wife.

The husband said, let us go down now and do what it is to make another come into the world.

Look, said the wife, the eternal clouds.

A Chair

A chair has waited such a long time to be with its person. Through shadow and fly buzz and the floating dust it has waited such a long time to be with its person.

What it remembers of the forest it forgets, and dreams of a room where it waits — Of the cup and the ceiling — Of the Animate One.

How a Cow Comes to Live with Long Eared Ones

A rabbit had killed a man in a wood one day. A cow watched waiting for the man to stand up. An insect crawled on the man's face. A cow watched waiting for the man to stand up. A cow jumped a fence to see closer how a rabbit does to a man. A rabbit attacks a cow thinking the cow may come to aid the man. The rabbit overcomes the cow and drags the cow down into its hole.

When the cow comes awake the cow thinks, I wish I was on top of the earth going with the man to my barn.

But the cow must remain with these long eared ones for the rest of its life.

Father Father, What Have You Done?

A man straddling the apex of his roof cries, giddyup. The house rears up on its back porch and all its bricks fall apart and the house crashes to the ground.

His wife cries from the rubble, father father, what have you done?

Of the Snake and the Horse

The snake is a thin beast, longer much than wide. Its head is a poisonous jewel. It comes to remind humankind that fear has form and evil shape, said father.

I like the horse so much better, father, said mother.

The horse has a human arse and a cow's head, said father.

And the horse tramples the snake, doesn't it, father, because the horse is on the side of humankind, isn't it, father? said mother.

The horse was invented by man after the horseless carriage; since the carriage was horseless they said let us invent a horse. At first the horseless carriages were afraid of the horses, mechanical things are terribly timid. But behind the invention lay the weapon that does the thin beast, longer much than wide, under its hooves, said father.

Was that how man was saved again to dwell in paradise, father? said mother, and why this is the best of all possible worlds?

This is the best of all possible worlds only because it is the only one that showed up, said father.

Shall we wait for the others? said mother.

Shall we wait for the others? . . . You stupid thing, said father.

A Machine

A man had built a machine.

. . . Which does what? said his father.

Which gets red with rust if it rains, wouldn't you say so, father?

But the machine is something to put a man out of work, said his father, and as work is prayer, so the machine is a damnation.

But the machine can also be sweethearts, growing cobwebs between its wheels where little black hands crawl; and soon the grasses come up between its gears — And its spokes laced with butterflies . . .

I do not like the machine, even if it is friendly, because it may yet decide to love my wife and take my bus to work, said the father.

No no, father, it is a flying machine.

Well, suppose the machine builds a nest on the roof and has baby machines? said the father.

Father, if you would only stare at the machine for a few hours you would learn to love it, to perhaps devote your very life to it.

I would not do no such a thing, not with your mother watching, itemizing my betrayals with which to confront me in bed . . . Perhaps I would soften toward this humble iron work, for even now I feel moved to assure it that there is a God, *yes, even for you, dear patient machine.* But your mother is watching. Even my mother is watching. All the women of the household are watching from the windows, waiting to see what I shall do.

But father, look at the dew on its wheels, does it not make you think of tears?

Would you break my heart whilst the women watch, half hoping that I shall weaken? for they are hungry for the victim that would be a kindness for me to deliver.

Then bow to the machine, father, be kind to the women as you are kind to the machine.

Oh no, dear child, I could not bow to a machine; I am, after all, human. Let others open new doors of history . . .

Waiting for the Signal Man

A woman said to her mother, where is my daughter?

Her mother said, up you and through me and out of grandmother; coming all the way down through all women like a railway train, trailing her brunette hair, which streams back grey into white; waiting for the signal man to raise his light so she can come through.

What she waiting for? said the woman.

For the signal man to raise his light, so she can see to come through.

The Fetcher of Wood

An old man got into a soup pot and shook a wooden spoon at the sky. When he had finished he went upstairs to his room and died.

When his wife came home she said, stop being dead, there is no reason for it.

He got out of bed. So you're dead, what of it? she said. I have no patience with you today — Go fetch wood for the stove.

He collapsed onto the floor. Oh, go along with you, you can at least fetch some wood. She kicked the corpse to the stairs and over the edge, and it fell to the first floor. Now, fetch wood, she screamed.

The corpse dragged itself out of the door. Spiteful old man, she said to herself, died just to get out of fetching wood.

The old man's cadaver was trying to chop wood. The ax kept slipping out of its hands. The cadaver had cut off one of its legs below the knee.

Now the cadaver came hopping on one leg into the kitchen, carrying its leg. Oh, you've cut my old man's leg off, she screamed. And she was so angry that she fetched the ax and began to chop up the corpse — Chop your leg off to get out of work, will you? — Die when I need you to bring the wood in, will you? . . .

The old man, leaning over a cloud, watched the old woman chopping up his corpse — Give it hell, baby, give it one for me . . .

When the old woman had finished, she gathered up the pieces and put them into a soup pot — Now die to your heart's content — And tell me you can't fetch wood . . .

23

Dinner Time

An old man sitting at table was waiting for his wife to serve dinner. He heard her beating a pot that had burned her. He hated the sound of a pot when it was beaten, for it advertised its pain in such a way that made him wish to inflict more of same. And he began to punch at his own face, and his knuckles were red. How he hated red knuckles, that blaring color, more self-important than the wound.

He heard his wife drop the entire dinner on the kitchen floor with a curse. For as she was carrying it in it had burned her thumb. He heard the forks and spoons, the cups and platters all cry at once as they landed on the kitchen floor. How he hated a dinner that, once prepared, begins to burn one to death, and as if that weren't enough, screeches and roars as it lands on the floor, where it belongs anyway.

He punched himself again and fell on the floor.

When he came awake again he was quite angry, and so he punched himself again and felt dizzy. Dizziness made him angry, and so he began to hit his head against the wall, saying, now get real dizzy if you want to get dizzy. He slumped to the floor.

Oh, the legs won't work, eh? . . . He began to punch his legs. He had taught his head a lesson and now he would teach his legs a lesson.

Meanwhile he heard his wife smashing the remaining dinnerware and the dinnerware roaring and shrieking.

He saw himself in the mirror on the wall. Oh, mock me, will you. And so he smashed the mirror with a chair, which broke. Oh, don't want to be a chair no more; too good to be sat on, eh? He began to beat the pieces of the chair.

He heard his wife beating the stove with an ax. He called, when're we going to eat? as he stuffed a candle into his mouth.

When I'm good and ready, she screamed.

Want me to punch your bun? he screamed.

Come near me and I'll kick an eye out of your head.

I'll cut your ears off.

I'll give you a slap right in the face.

I'll break you in half.

The old man finally ate one of his hands. The old woman said, damn fool, whyn't you cook it first? you go on like a beast — You know I have to subdue the kitchen every night, otherwise it'll cook me and serve me to the mice on my best china. And you know what small eaters they are; next would come the flies, and how I hate flies in my kitchen.

The old man swallowed a spoon. Okay, said the old woman, now we're short one spoon.

The old man, growing angry, swallowed himself.

Okay, said the woman, now you've done it.

A Red Mustache

A heavy woman with a rolling pin said, I am the king.

A fly lighted on her nose. She hit the fly on her nose with her rolling pin. Do not disturb her highness with trivialities, she said, as the blood from her nose formed a red mustache.

Darling, said her husband, you have a red mustache.

The woman who is king backed up.

Her husband watched her red mustache.

The woman who is king came forward.

Her husband watched her red mustache and said, darling, what's with the red mustache?

I am king of everything, she said, I am king Mama.

And the rolling pin, dearest? he said.

Is the scepter of brutality, she said.

And the apron and the hair in its greasy little bun? he said.

Which is the fortress and the image that people shall come to fear, she said.

And the red mustache, so outlandish on a fat middle-aged hausfrau? he said.

The red mustache which you constantly refer to is the sign of office, the change of gender, the self inflicted blow, the secondary hair of my manhood, the end of my menopause, the return to maidenhood, the cerebral menses from my nose instead of my under part . . . , she said.

But what about the red mustache? he said.

If you really must know I killed a fly on my nose with a rolling pin, she said.

No you didn't, he's flying around on the ceiling, he said.

Oh look, he's on your head, she said.

Hold it, he screamed.

I must kill it, she said.

No, don't, he screamed.

It'll get on my nose, she said.

Oh please clean the blood off your face and cook dinner, he screamed.

Oh oh oh, she cried, I do not know what to do. Oh oh oh . . .

Wash your face, he said.

No, that is not a thing to do, oh oh oh, she cried.

Well what is it, suddenly, with that red mustache? he said.

Oh I want to be loved more than all things else, oh oh oh . . . , she cried.

Appearance

There was a landscape once in a while where a rock a person and a pebble and will it rain one day, gathered one day to appear.

There was a landscape that became a room to search for a house, to decide to stay there, then to be old in a house it finds.

And so the sun came in a room's window and woke a person who poured coffee out of a cup into his head.

A Man Who Writes

A man had written *head* on his forehead, and *hand* on each hand, and *foot* on each foot.

His father said, stop stop stop, because the redundancy is like having two sons, which is two sons too many, as in the first instance which is one son too many.

The man said, may I write *father* on father?
Yes, said father, because one father is tired of bearing it all alone.

Mother said, I'm leaving if all these people come to dinner.
But the man wrote *dinner* all over the dinner.

When dinner was over father said to his son, will you write *belch* on my belch?

The man said, I will write *God bless everyone* on God.

Love

Dog, love me, said a man to a dog. A dog said nothing.

But a piece of glass when properly with the sun glittered into his eye — I hear you, said the man.

But a leaf wristing on its stem because the wind wanted to go someplace, turned the man to itself — So you are saying such and such, he said.

He noticed wrinkles on his shoe — Muscle stretch which is what a smile is; my shoe is smiling at me. Shoe, I love you, love me. But his shoe merely walked on, his head hovering above it . . .

Head, head, love me, he said to his head.

His head had a nostril. He felt it. There were two. One nostril must have had a baby.

But his nostril blew air at his fingers.

I can blow air at a nostril too. So he screwed up his lips and blew air at his nostrils.

The Definition

He that puts suicide into his left ear pretends it is wax. His mother says, but it's a bullet which you have shot yourself with.

Is that how I died? he said.

That's when the funeral began, it was like a flower festival; your father asked me to marry him, and with much declining as to appear of greater value I agreed. Of the two of us, your father and I, so overlapping we blurred into three. I said, how is this? Your father said, this is this. And this was you. But for a time we could not tell who any of us were. Your father said, who am I? And I said, am I you? And he said, if you are me then I am the small one there and the small one is you. And after much declining I agreed to be anyone; I said, someone is passing the house, shall I be someone passing the house? . . . and so forth. Until we discovered that we had shadows; so that in the morning we would assemble and let the sun stencil us on the wall: The largest of the three we allowed would be the father, the next largest, the mother, and the smallest, the third one, which you were called as we did not know who you were . . . And that you might be a wood god or the spirit of the house . . . So that we allowed you to define yourself.

But of my suicide? . . .

But you see that is another definition of the first turning which was turned when I wasn't looking . . .

And of my death? . . .

As a festival of flowers . . . declining as to appear of greater value . . .

A Stone Is Nobody's

A man ambushed a stone. Caught it. Made it a prisoner. Put it in a dark room and stood guard over it for the rest of his life.

His mother asked why.

He said, because it's held captive, because it is the captured.

Look, the stone is asleep, she said, it does not know whether it's in a garden or not. Eternity and the stone are mother and daughter; it is you who are getting old. The stone is only sleeping.

But I caught it, mother, it is mine by conquest, he said.

A stone is nobody's, not even its own. It is you who are conquered; you are minding the prisoner, which is yourself, because you are afraid to go out, she said.

Yes yes, I am afraid, because you have never loved me, he said.

Which is true, because you have always been to me as the stone is to you, she said.

Fire Is Not a Nice Guest

I had charge of an insane asylum, as I was insane.

A fire came, which got hungry; so I said, you may eat a log, but do not go upstairs and eat a dementia praecox.

I said, insane people, go into the attic while a fire eats a kitchen chair for breakfast.

But fire wanted a kitchen curtain, which it ate and climbed at the same time, and went then into the ceiling to eat a rafter.

I said, if you're so hungry eat a rafter, but do not eat a maniac.

Meanwhile, a maniac in the attic, with a hatchet, began to attack the sky.

You'll make it rain, you do that, I said, you'll wound it to rain.

The fire was eating an old lady. I said, one old lady, yes, and a child for dessert.

I said to the fire that it may take a siesta in the maniac's bed. But the fire wanted to eat the bed. You are too hungry, fire, I said. But, by that time the fire's whole family had moved in, and was eating out the corners of the asylum — Hey, that's where the dusts have built their cities.

But the fires will not listen as they do not like to starve.

So I called the lunatics out of the attic and said to them that this is a war of nutrition, and that they must eat the fire, which, if not, will eat them.

But they said, we are not fire-eaters, we are sword-swallowers . . .

Little Dead Man

Onward, little dead man, said a little man passing through a land of butterflies, purple and white, yellow and black, all in flux; they are not told from the flowers they drink, nor are the wind fluttered flowers from those they host.

This is a land of vibrating velvet. Eating itself. Forming itself. This is the land of death. Endless. Absurd.

A Child Walking Out Of a Cow's Behind

A door would wish to swing out upon its hinges . . . But no one comes, said an old woman looking at a door with binoculars from a tree. A door is the difference between in and out.

A cow is eating a child. No, a child is passing behind a cow.

One can see. One looks. Yet one cannot see what is behind the door.

I believe a cow is eating a child. No, a child is passing behind a cow.

What if once on the other side of the door there remains only the urgency to use the door again?

Do my binoculars entitle me to know something?

Were I a door I would wish to swing out upon my hinges, and allow my room to fill with what has come from the outside.

Is that cow eating a child?

Now I see a child walking out of a cow's behind.

Rat

In a shack on the wall was a tree in a window. But here lived a rat. A rat is not tall enough to see a tree from a window, that a rat must go out of doors entirely and say, I see a tree.

Now where the rat was a man was. Where a man was a rat was to be. No one said, hello rat, because no one said, hello.

A rat's tail is a rat's tail. A rat-tail is dragged by the dragger who is a rat. (Rats travel by boat which is so much better than swimming, and good eats are had at sea).

It is lonely, but a rat is busy being a rat. Every day the rat forms itself into a rat.

In the vicinity the moon was seen if anything decided to name it. The window flows to the floor on a ray of moon. Time in silvered light.

Does a rat act for all rats? A rat drags a rat-tail, for all rats, to a dead moth who is dead as all moths are or will be, and eats the moth, its wings and antennae . . .

A rat is not a rat unless a rat climbs out of itself and sees a rat. And even then a rat might say: I'm a Maryanne, the daughter of man.

A rat has no chance of being a rat, until the great God says, arise rat, thou art a rat; thou art come to be that which thou namest thyself after the name I give thee . . .

In the Time of Commerce

Between the man and the woman is part of the man, which has been thought to be part of the woman, given to the man to be given back to the woman in the time of their commerce.

The window is described by moonlight on the further wall.

Paying the Captain

We get on a boat, never mind if it sinks, we pay the captain by throwing him overboard. And when he gets back onboard we say, captain, please don't be angry. And he forgives us this time. And so we throw him overboard again just to make sure we have fully paid the price we have set upon our passage. When he gets back onboard he is not anxious to forgive us, and he would like it much better if we would get off his boat. There is nothing left for us to do but to repay him and hope that this time it will be enough. And so we throw him overboard again. When he comes aboard again we say, now this must be the last of this, we will pay no more, we want the journey to begin.

But it seems there will be no journey since we have gotten the captain used to a good thing. And so we must spend the rest of our days throwing the captain overboard.

Dark Friends

One who is now in proximity to a door decides that he shall open a door and step into the place that the door is entrance to.

After he closes a door, which he is now doing, he will've come where he must decide again. As he sits behind the door the decision forms; so that he rises and opens the door again and passes out from the place of his last deciding.

His mother says, don't be coming in and out, the flies follow you.

They are dark friends buzzing something of song and something of wisdom; friendly ones against whom the woman of the house has set her hand. They are the people of wings.

Again he would have to do with the door. The decision made. The passage accomplished. Point of rest, and the decision again being made. Made. And the passage . . .

His mother said, either stay in or stay out; the house is full of flies.

One who is now in proximity breaks this proximity and is flying and buzzing away with a host of dark friends who are buzzing and flying.

II

from
What A Man Can See

1969

What a Man Can See

There was a tower where a man said I can live. After grief it can happen that he comes. Then he saw summer its field and its tree. He heard the wind and he saw a cloud.

The Road

There was a road that leads him to go to find a certain time where he sits.

Smokes quietly in the evening by the four legged table wagging its (well why not) tail, friendly chap.

Hears footsteps, looks to find his own feet gone.

The road absorbs everything with rumors of sleep.

And then he looked for himself and even he was gone.

— Looked for the road and even that . . .

There Was

A man who said lobster when a basket was in a house, where a child eats an orange to please a ceiling, or dreams and dies.

There was an orange that had a dream in a fruitbowl, the orange dreamed that at the age of puberty life is very good when it is.

The man said lobster when a basket was in a house, but secretly removed by agents of the statue which stood quietly in the square.

The ceiling pleased grew displeased and then grew pleased again.

To have said lobster when a basket is not in a house is to have said lobster when a basket is not in a house, he did not like to say lobster when a basket is not in a house.

The ceiling was quite displeased and so it grew pleased again.

In a house there was once a child who was eaten by an orange, or did it dream and die.

The agents of the statue secretly removed the ceiling as it slumbered in the afternoon.

Once upon a time there was a room where an orange and a basket and a ceiling lived, this room took up residence in a house as it is better than to be living in a forest where you cannot be cheerful anymore.

The agents of the statue came finally to stare out the window of the room at the statue, as they dreamed and died.

There was an eaten who was oranged by a child to ceiling a please and a lobster that said basket when a house was in a man.

Memory and the Sun

There was once a memory of a person that would not go even though a person had said I do not like memories and died, for there was a habit that needed badly to be repeated.

A woman saw the sunshine coming in a window looking through a memory to find a person to form a shadow.

He did not like memories or old persons he said, he did not like a habit which is brown in a cup and a cigarette turning to smoke.

He did not like the sun to repeat him on the wall or the woman to repeat him by name.

The sun annoys the woman that it should search the room everyday lighting the wall where he had cursed his shadow. The sun comes everyday because it has become used to coming through a window where it rests safely in its golden gloom. The vain sunlight lying on the floor sunning itself, a yellow kitten made of dust.

He had not liked old persons who had become more memory than flesh sitting in the sun like peopleless shadows.

It

It was someone as viewed in a mirror, or was it you said it was some-one viewing its someone who it is in a mirror where perhaps someone lives only.

Someone is not the chair but part of where, where a table and a blue in square is a window and some sky.

Nor is the chair someone with someone on its lap.

Someone becomes embarrassed sitting on a chair's lap. Who is person who allows person this intimacy. It is none but man's form. Is not sir said son of a mother to himself the son of his mother. Did not the chair make me to warm itself like I am a blanket for a chair.

The mirror is willing to allow anything to be — Creates to-be again.

Time is passing.

Time has passed.

And then time is passing.

Passed, it begins to pass again.

The Man Rock

A man is a rock in a garden of chairs and waits for a longtime to be over.

It is easier for a rock in a garden than a man inside his mother. He decided to be a rock when he got outside.

A rock asks only what is a rock.

A rock waits to be a rock.

A rock is a longtime waiting for a longtime to be over so that it may turn and go the other way.

A rock awakens into a man. A man looks. A man sleeps back into a rock as it is better for a rock in a garden than a man inside himself trembling in red darkness.

Mr Is

Mr Is' head was made of wood. He had become like a man with a wooden leg. His head was now auxiliary.

One day he noticed this as he was trying to think of mother. One day he was trying to think of mother and he noticed that his head had become wood. He tried to think of mother but his head had became quite wooden.

He put hats on his head. He put a homburg on the head. He put a peaked cap on it. He put Aunt Mill's lace doily on it.

He could not think anymore.

He said, I am done with thought.

He thought, I have no thoughts.

Unlovely bushes of hair grew out of the head which he kept cropped like the hedge around mother's house.

Mr Is went into the woods to think about his wooden head.

In the woods is where you think good because it is getting close to nature and therefore you can think better.

Mr Brain

Mr Brain was a hermit dwarf who liked to eat shellfish off the moon. He liked to go into a tree then because there is a little height to see a little further, which may reveal now the stone, a pebble — it is a twig, it is nothing under the moon that you can make sure of.

So Mr Brain opened his mouth to let a moonbeam into his head.

Why to be alone, and you invite the stars to tea. A cup of tea drinks a luminous guest.

In the winter could you sit quietly by the window, in the evening when you could have vinegar and pretend it to be wine, because you would do well to eat doughnuts and pretend you drink wine as you sit quietly by the window. You may kick your leg back and forth. You may have a tendency to not want to look there too long and turn to find darkness in the room because it had become nighttime.

Why to be alone. You are pretty are you not/you are as pretty as you are not, or does that make sense.

You are not pretty, that is how you can be alone. And then you are pretty like fungus and alga, you are no one without some one, in theory alone.

Be good enough to go to bed so you can not think too much longer.

A Man With a Tree on His Head

A man had been married to a woman's high-heeled shoe for seven years.

He did not like to be spoken to because it confused the hair on his head which had a tendency to become grass when ever it tended that way, which it was anyway, which he hid under wild flowers he let grow in his part, hiding those under bushes growing from the back of his head, topped finally by a cherrytree from which he ate as opposed to starving to death.

He would wrap his wife in newspaper whenever he did so.
If he heard a street noise he heard a street noise.
If he heard a cow moo he heard a cow moo and that settled it, it was not a dog barking. Or was it. Or a dog learned to speak cow. Or a cow pretending to be a dog speaking cow — And something very much to think about.

A cloud was once in the sky as he remembers and he looked up at it, or was it a cow barking.

The shoe asked him to leave the house and he did so and snuck back through a window and watched the shoe going to the bathroom.

Mrs Reach Reached Into the Air

I cannot reach higher than there, she roared. That is quite high, said Mr Reach, high enough to hang clothes on a washline, to put cupboards in shape by arranging the crocks and box. But can it be high enough to be high enough, she screamed. It can be high enough to be low enough if you'll stoop to clean floors, said Mr Reach. Is that where they are, she screamed. You're standing on one, he said. But I'm trying to do upwards, to get going, to reach into the reachiest reach, she roared. Stop doing such as you do because I get nervous when you do such and such, he said. I can do it too many times if so to choose I choose to do it, she screamed. Stop stop before you cannot do it more, because it is better to be able to do it more than to do it more and not be able to do it anymore, he said. But my arms have got long like I could be an ape if so I wanted, and so I want to be an ape, she screamed. You will go to a zoo ladyloo because your mind is full of monkey fur, he said. It is not it is full of goods, to be opened posthumously, she roared. Stop stop, he said, the floor has a dirt on it, your arms must come out of heaven — Oh please let them come out of heaven so I may slap their hands. I am shaking hands with several angels and it tickles like don't tickle me or I'll scream, she screamed. Oh it is getting to very not nice, he said.

And so Mrs Reach reached into the air.

The Lover

The lover has four legs and it loves itself the hairy pits of its arms and legs.

The lover has four arms and sleeps all tangled in its persons, all hands on skin and up backside through hair up belly a handful of breast the neck is sweet and the ear is kissed and the eye is kissed and the mouth licked.

And then sick of it all and a bird sings and the wallpaper hums with the monotony of a flower who is monotonous all over the walls.

The lover is two having coffee midsummer by a window, nude white ones in afternoon light full of twigs, a tree by the window.

Dream Man

Dream man said he will do dreams. He has a box and a clock. He has a clock to wind when it is Wednesday.

An apple is very cherry bigger, it is very something the same.

And dream man said he will do dreams, he will do boxes — Now can you hide there, yes you can. And the clock which can go tick.

If somebody who loves you does not love you and there is very nothing to do like you will wind on Wednesday or apple as a cherry is as is an apple as a cherry.

Can you hide, I think so. Can you think so, I think so. In a box to hide. Can you do a box like you can a dream if somebody who loves you does not love you.

You can do a dream like she loves you.

Dream man will dream he is not dreaming and dream himself awake and wind his clock which makes it Wednesday and he has a box.

A Person

A person lived with a window and wall, tea pot and cup, table and chair.

A person's mother on visit said get up. A person got up to stand by the window. The mother said goodbye and left. A person sat down again.

There was a tree where a bird was, of the window, and kept a person company or parallel. And a bird flies and so it returns to a tree where a bird was.

Taking tea a person takes tea and to watch pleasantly the bird and the day is not badly spent. And more tea as there is no limit to the indulgence when an afternoon is not too bright as it may rain, as sweet cobwebs lull with no little love the timid mouse of the heart.

Grey is the light and a green tree there and the ceiling asleep, a cobweb puts the ceiling to asleep.

Then dead persons on a washline in wind that is before it will rain.

Table with a drawer. In the drawer there lives a spool of thread with a kitchen knife and a nutcracker and a rubberband to be touched during days spent seeking essence.

Hair can be touched, one does not know if it has color, on a day before it will rain hair may get grey, as if strings of rain out of the head.

An orange is color of a bright orange before it rains. The orange is then alone. I do not like alone, as it is cozy I admit but too perfected in a round orange of that color.

The ceiling snores, it is a lovely place, I think of all things I love the ceiling best.

The floor has a certain way to live by itself, though with us it will not join me for tea as the tree and some of the air will, which is welcome but to disturb not any of the dusts in their lays and joyous charities to my soul.

I see mother in air coming hooked to a basket of oranges. Her hair is white as is her face, wearing grey as air is. Is it mother or air or the blooming of an orangetree.

It is mother coming nearer.

Without tree where a bird was as now a mother to occupy the window, and the ceiling purring in this while, and mother through the window at me looking as I can see a cobweb gently nodding, and I take its mild approach and keep my face so that it can appreciate that my eyes are for it only.

The huge one with a basket of oranges and a lace collar, becoming no doubt if the eye was allowed to weave only in little eyelets of lace, to appreciate as foam may teach, dear me along the beach. Or wearing bright brass policeman buttons, or a tunic of birds and a waist band of fawn pipes so it seems, and wearing a shawl of father shackled to her neck, dead I believe but lifted by wind.

Through the window onto the kitchen table, a table with a drawer in which living does a spool with its delicious thread, neighbored with a kitchen knife and a good friend a nutcracker side by side with a rubber band.

Mother said stand up. And then mother said stoop.

The ceiling does not, cannot, like mother and I concur.

The floor has been spared mother as she stands on the table, where now she dances giving an attractive display of ladies' high laced boots in motion, less soft than the cobweb's motion, she quicker than and less with love.

Her oranges come jumping from their basket skipping to the table and down to the floor, and now the floor must feel as it must as it receives these new ones with certain gracious flights of dust disturbed and politely moving.

Mother decides to sit on the table and stare at me for the rest of my life, which is not to see a tree where a bird was, and her policeman buttons seem so angry, I am sure we shall be friends as they tarnish so sweetly. Did not a spoon come with very brightness not to friendship, soon to tarnish and to love. Yes the teaspoon clothed in mirror, and soon to love, took friends of tea stain and dust, but the tarnish meant such much.

I did not live long as mother walked through my breast and out the door to the rear where I never look as it takes turning as I never.

I heard the dusts never too bitter rise in her passage and come resting to the floor with certain socially agreeable comments which makes life so much something or other, but it is very nice to know the community, or something like that as mother puts it, or has put it, hidden it no doubt that I might rise and discover it for myself which is not likely anymore because it is quite unlikely that I shall be forced to overflow my borders with any sudden distaste that might arrive surreptitiously in the night on the wings of some indigestible tidbit that turns as I shall not to be a seed of some tree that aspires through my limbs parasitically, for I have not the strength to use or to be done with.

There was a stone once that I knew of whom certain persons had asked to join a certain violence. The stone refused to give itself or to refuse itself, not that it ever came to the point of actual refusal, the stone merely shut its eyes and remained silent, and for all I may ever know the stone is still living with some grass, or is it a shadow that said hello.

It is possible to sit in a chair.

The Fall

There was a man who found two leaves and came indoors holding them out saying to his parents that he was a tree.

To which they said then go into the yard and do not grow in the living-room as your roots may ruin the carpet.

He said I was fooling I am not a tree and he dropped his leaves.

But his parents said look it is fall.

Signs

As he said his ghost person self was not to be loved too much as it was a ghost person and that he was not himself anymore since the puppet master was making him a vicarious person in a house full of signs.

A certain cup in arrangement with a spoon and a doily contrived a certain mood that all will be well if you hold your breath for the count of three.

There was also a huge face on mother's back which was her real face. The other little face was a phoney little face that pretends kindness on the front of her head. The huge face looks at one as mother pretends to be washing dishes at the sink, it is the big ugly man that looks out of her back, her apron tied in the back to effect a bow tie effect for the big ugly man.

As the flesh and bones under the skin had become water and drained out of the big toe and one was empty one had been forced to submit to bamboo rods which were forced through the tips of the fingers up the arms as through the toes into the legs.

One tries to concentrate on the small effects which try to speak in a quiet way, small scenes like the corner of a room arranging itself to speak in symbol with its little table flanked by a meaningful shadow and some small colonies of dust.

Then again when his mother climbed on his shoulders her skirts all up around his head, and sat there moaning, he could not tell whether his mother was being borne by him or he being born by her.

To Be of Some Use

If the head could be converted into a sort of shack for animals one might turn a pretty penny, small animals that profit one their eggs and fur, as one must leave and so make certain business arrangements.

There was a certain stone that did very well in the middle of a wood, but then that is not for me.

As a child I had wanted to become an automobile, but then I grew up to be 30 years old.

To do useful work like lifting one's hand into the air and pinching the underside of a cloud.

The walking of the black squares on the linoleum in mother's kitchen might be turned to profit, say by hooking a string to one's ear which could be attached in a distant city to a dummy's mouth, or across the Atlantic to a Dutch windmill on a day when there is little wind.

Or a yawn might be used as a prelude to sleep.

I said to mother the head might be used to keep tropical fish in, and one might carve out a small income — a mailorder business so to speak, mailing oneself in a coffin — saving the costs of a book-keeper by, so to speak, having the business in one's head.

Mother slapped me across my mouth, which one is hard put to interpret.

Not to feel too useless these days I keep myself busy smoking cigarettes and drinking coffee. I am not against spending my time sleeping just as long as I am doing something with my time.

Had I more arms and legs I would seriously consider becoming the frame for an umbrella — with some sexual arousement my penis could be used as the handle — Is it not already used to help old ladies up and down stairs.

Sometimes I just breathe. Did you ever do that. I say to mother, look I am breathing.

I get little recognition — or mother is scanty with praise only that I might not rest on my laurels — that I will keep a firm and steady gaze into the darkness that others choose to call the future.

I seek a land where I might become of some use — or rather my use might come to some recognition — that in other words, mother might come eventually to write her congressman of my worth — and that the daily papers might be filled with picture stories, titled: He Smokes A Cigarette — He Can Breathe — Etc. And that crowds might stand outside the house cheering me as I sleep.

Perhaps I should kiss the face of the kitchen clock for luck. Perhaps its little hands with rapture would encircle my neck, and we might be happy.

I am sure happiness is not too far away.

Through the Woods

There was a woman who sits in a chair and becomes welded to it, and to further herself on any path she tilts and rocks — like, to have tea, I don't mind if I do, from kettle to teapot and oh me to teacup and back for sugar and then to find lemons or is it milk or cream, the saucer is missing and then the tea is cold, and lemon is better if so I wish which I do not as I wish for milk or is it cream, or would I best appease myself with lemon, which is all to be had on the kitchen table which I cannot find, nor can I the kitchen or its house.

So she had to go through the woods tilting and rocking her chair through leaf and vine. Why am I going where I cannot tell the time of day. Because that is where they said hello to Matthew. Which is not the answer said her head. So she had to go through the woods sitting on her chair.

And then there was a kitchen with a kitchen table with no lady sitting on a chair. So the kitchen had to go through the woods because where else can a kitchen go when it decides.

The woman who sits on a chair and the kitchen saw each other as each supposed the other didn't and each decided to hide from the other as it was for each a quaint jest deserving no further mention save that neither ever found either, and it is sad indeed to go through the woods never finding.

Father and Son Travelling

A man had a sack which he kept father in. As he stood in the doorway of mother's house in silhouette with the sack over his shoulder, mother said, I see you are humpbacked, which is well, like the mother is the son, a flattery which is also echoed in our chin hairs, in our similar balding.

No, no, mother, my humped back is father . . .

Yes, your father was a humpback with chin hair, bald because he is of the family, flattering me by every loss and gain of his aging body; when his hair went so went mine, it was a morning not quite like this night, yet not quite dissimilar to be that different; but to go on, we had been sleeping, yes, and weeping, as was our way, also reaping, as was our way, the harvest that the dream is yielding; but when the morning came we found all our lovely hair on the pillow. It is my hair, said your father, as he gathered it up and spilled it on his head. And then the door opened and the wind came in and gathered it like a tumble weed and took it away. We stood at the door and watched the lovely silver stuff go down the road.

But I have father here in this sack, we have been travelling.

How nice for father and son to find the earth round or flat, or how you say, humpback, growing your chin hair, no matter where, it keeps coming out like your whole head was full of it.

Father wishes to blow you a kiss through the sack.

Wait son, I shall have to put some underwear over my face to keep discretion and modesty, while well admitting it is most flattering to have a person with chin hair demonstrate his affection . . . I think it better though if he did nothing, rather thought of my nude body discreetly inside his head.

He is now thinking of your nakedness, mother, which is a fine picture for the father to take on the road as he travels with the son. Goodbye, mother.

Yes, yes, goodbye, hello . . .

One Two Three, One Two Three

A clock has twelve numbers — Father, the clock has twelve numbers, and I have ten fingers, which equals twenty two things — Father, father, mother has two eyes which I saw with my two eyes, which is four eyes . . .

Will you stop counting on things. They never turn out when you count on them, said father.

Father, you have two eyes which with my fingers is twelve, said the son.

The old man said to his wife, will you make him stop counting, because it's like having bugs crawling on everything.

I can't, because he do it in his head where I can't make him stop. He do it like in secret, said the old woman.

Why do he have to be so secret, asked the old man.

Because he have a funny shaped head, she answered.

The old man said to his son: Why have you got a funny shaped head.

So I can wear little hats instead of big father-hats.

But you bigger'n me already, and you still wearing little hats. Ain't you never going to wear a big people's hat, said the old man.

Father, I have one head, I counted it, screamed the son.

Mother, said the old man, make him stop having secrets.

I can't because his secrets inside his head, she said.

Well maybe if we have dinner he'll put food in his mouth so he can't tell his secrets, the old man said.

We having your favorite because we ain't got nothing else, which is just as well because it's your favorite anyway, she said.

What we having, he asked.

One two three, one two three, father, screamed the son.

We having, said the old woman, water and love.

Their son said: Water & Love & my head equals three.

That's poor folks' food; they lives on love. I'd rather have some of your nightgowns—Why don't you make some nightgown stew, and you could throw the boy's photograph in for flavor, said the old man.

I'm going to my room, we'll have dinner tomorrow night, she said.

I don't care, go to bed forever for all I care—Your son's got a bullet-head, shouted the old man.

Look out father, or I'll shoot you, screamed their son.

He's going to shoot me with his bullet-head, the old man said.

Well be damned you old fucker, his wife screamed.

III

from
The Clam Theater

1973

The Agent

. . . Assigned to you when your flesh was separating from your mother's, this shadow, who seeing the opportunity at hand, joined your presence in such a way as some say the soul is given.

You have always caricatured me in my travels. I have seen you on mountains, and in dim cafes. I have seen you hold your head, your elbows on your knees; and while I was sad you were serene!

I seek a mastery over fate, of which you are, in objective witness, the agent of . . . I run away one night as you sleep, the trusting wife, whose borders have opened in the universal dark.

She feels in the morning among the sheets for the easy habit of her husband's shape — Now arc the earth, sweet dark, the law of umbra give you panic to search me out with your cunning speed of light!

The Ancestral Mousetrap

We are left a mousetrap, baited with cheese. We must not jar it, or our ancestor's gesture and pressure are lost, as the trap springs shut.

He has relinquished his hands to what the earth makes of flesh. Still, here in this mousetrap is caught the thumb print of his pressure.

A mouse would steal this with its death, this still unspent jewel of intent.

In a jewel box it is kept, to keep it from the robber-mouse; even as memory in the skull was kept, to keep it from the robber-worm, who even now is climbing a thief in the window of his eyes.

The Ant Farm

In spite even of Columbus the world collapses and goes flat again.
The sky is a bell jar where a child in another scale watches his ant farm.
When the bored child yawns two thousand years pass.

Someday we have crashed to the playroom floor; the careless child knocks us over with his fire truck . . . All that dirt lying in its broken sky.
Swept up, it is thrown into a garbage can at the back of the universe.

Ape and Coffee

Some coffee had gotten on a man's ape. The man said, animal did you get on my coffee?

No no, whistled the ape, the coffee got on me.

You're sure you didn't spill on my coffee? said the man.

Do I look like a liquid? peeped the ape.

Well you sure don't look human, said the man.

But that doesn't make me a fluid, twittered the ape.

Well I don't know what the hell you are, so just stop it, cried the man.

I was just sitting here reading the newspaper when you splashed coffee all over me, piped the ape.

I don't care if you are a liquid, you just better stop splashing on things, cried the man.

Do I look fluid to you? Take a good look, hooted the ape.

If you don't stop I'll put you in a cup, screamed the man.

I'm not a fluid, screeched the ape.

Stop it, stop it, screamed the man, you are frightening me.

The Blank Book

The book was blank, all the words had fallen out.

Her husband said, the book is blank.

His wife said, a funny thing happened to me on my way to the present moment. I was shaking the book, to get all the typos out, and all of a sudden all the words and punctuation fell out too. Maybe the whole book was a typo?

And what did you do with the words? said her husband.

I made a package and mailed it to a fictitious address, she said.

But no one lives there. Don't you know, hardly anyone lives at fictitious addresses. There's barely enough reality there to provide even a mailing address, he said.

That's why I sent them there. Words all mixed up can suddenly coalesce into rumors and malicious gossip, she said.

But don't these blank pages also present a dangerous invitation to rumors and malicious gossip? Who knows what anyone might write in his absent-mindedness? Who knows what chance might do with such a dangerous invitation? he said.

Perhaps we shall have to send ourselves away to some fictitious address, she said.

Is it because words keep falling out of our mouths, words that could easily start rumors and malicious gossip? he said.

It is because, somehow, we keep falling out of ourselves, like detached shadows; shaking as if we could get all the typos out of our lives, she said.

Well, at least, if this doesn't hurt reality, it does, in fact, give reality a well earned rest.

The Case

Your case . . . ?

Mine, which is the only excuse I give for opening it.

You are opening it.

Yes, it is opened by me, which is the only excuse I give for opening it.

And it has things inside of it . . .

Yes, things are inside because I have put them there, each in its own recess.

Instruments?

Yes, an old shoe which people will say is simply an old shoe. It is in my case to associate its presence with this gingerbread man . . . Then too, this rock, which is also to be noticed . . . And this toy sailboat . . .

These are things in your case.

These are things in my case. When I close my case they are still there. When I open my case I can see that. Because they are there they have probably been there all the time the case was closed . . . I guess at this. I am confident that I shall not reverse my opinion. I am very well satisfied that what I have believed is so. I have made no contingency plans.

Then you are sure?

I am filled with confidence. I am closing my case because I have finished having it open. I am relatching its latch because I have concluded its excuse for being open by closing it.

Then it's closed . . . ?

Yes, because I have done that to it.

The Changeling

A man had a son who was an anvil. And then sometimes he was an automobile tire.

I do wish you would sit still, said the father.

Sometimes his son was a rock.

I realize that you have quite lost boundary, where no excess seems excessive, nor to where poverty roots hunger to need. But should you allow time to embrace you to its bosom of dust, that velvet sleep, then were you served even beyond your need; and desire in sate was properly spilling from its borders, said the father.

Then his son became the corner of a room.

Don't don't, cried the father.

And then his son became a floorboard.

Don't don't, the moon falls there and curdles your wits into the grain of the wood, cried the father.

What shall I do? screamed his son.

Sit until time embraces you into the bosom of its velvet quiet, cried the father.

Like this? cried his son as his son became dust.

Ah, that is more pleasant, and speaks well of him, who having required much in his neglect of proper choice, turns now, on good advice, to a more advantageous social stance, said the father.

But then his son became his father.

Behold, the son is become as one of us, said the father.

His son said, behold, the son is become as one of us.

Will you stop repeating me, screamed the father.

Will you stop repeating me, screamed his son.

Oh well, I suppose imitation is the sincerest form of flattery, sighed the father.

Oh well, I suppose imitation is the sincerest form of flattery, sighed his son.

The Clam Theater

They had started a hat factory . . . Basically in a dream . . . Entirely so when you think that the very foundation begins somewhere in the brain, when the brain is unlaced like a shoe, and like a shoe free of the conscious foot with its corns and calls.

An old brick factory full of men mad for making hats rises in the head like Atlantis once more above the waters . . . It is remarkable how like a foot the head really is; I mean the toes, perhaps ornaments of hair; the hollow of the arch must certainly find its mouth, the heel is already a jaw . . .

This is my theater. I sit in my head asleep. Theater in a clam . . .

Amidst the wet flesh of the head madmen build hats; perhaps to lay cover over the broken mind; or to say the head is gone, and all it is is hat . . . Only hats hung on the hooks of our necks . . .

The Death of Dentistry

For some reason there was a vein of teeth that had developed without jaw or appetite in the earth, like precious stones or metals.

The toothless came here to bite the earth and to come away with teeth stabbed into their gums.

No telling what one would come up with, tusks, tiny mouse teeth . . . A toothless man no longer toothless cried through hippopotamus teeth, I have got myself handsome with a smile full of hippopotamus teeth!

Ah, but teeth are designed to a diet. He with cows' teeth ate grass saying, I do not like grass, but I eat grass because it fits my teeth. A cripple who must wear an ugly shoe; never mind the glass slipper. If the shoe fits, wear it.

And so they wore their teeth like shoes. Many allowing this wisdom walked on their teeth. Others, moving one more step in logic, kicked their feet into the earth, driving teeth into their feet.

These are funny shoes, said some, but if the shoe fits . . .

Others began to chew their food by stamping on it.

And so they came one more step in logic, and stuffed shoes in their mouths, crying, we have got leather teeth.

It was terrible that dentistry had come so far only to die at the foot of human logic.

The Difficulty With a Tree

A woman was fighting a tree. The tree had come to rage at the woman's attack, breaking free from its earth it waddled at her with its great root feet.

Goddamn these sentiencies, roared the tree with birds shrieking in its branches.

Look out, you'll fall on me, you bastard, screamed the woman as she hit at the tree.

The tree whisked and whisked with its leafy branches.

The woman kicked and bit screaming, kill me kill me or I'll kill you!

Her husband seeing the commotion came running crying, what tree has lost patience?

The ax the ax, damnfool, the ax, she screamed.

Oh no, roared the tree dragging its long roots rhythmically limping like a sea lion towards her husband.

But oughtn't we to talk about this? cried her husband.

But oughtn't we to talk about this, mimicked his wife.

But what is this all about? he cried.

When you see me killing something you should reason that it will want to kill me back, she screamed.

But before her husband could decide what next action to perform the tree had killed both the wife and her husband.

Before the woman died she screamed, now do you see?

He said, what . . . ? And then he died.

The Dog's Music

The rich hire orchestras, and have the musicians climb into trees to sit in the branches among the leaves, playing Happy Birthday to their dogs.

When the manservants come with birthday cakes, they are told, not now, do not dare disturb me when I am listening to my dog's music.

I was just wondering, sir, if I should light the candles?

I said not now. Do you want to distract me from my dog's music? Don't you realize that this is his birthday, and that it's been a whole year since his last birthday?

Shall I just put the cake in his feeding bowl, sir?

You are still distracting me from my dog's music. I wonder why you do it. This is not your birthday. Why are you trying to attract my attention?

But, sir, the cake . . .

But do you think I want my dog to see me talking to you while his music is being played? How would it seem to you if I talked to the dog while your music was being played?

So sorry, sir. I'll take the cake back to the house . . .

Oh no, it's gone too far for that — Sic'em, sic'em, cry the rich to their dogs.

And so the dogs of the rich leap on the serving men, who cry, help help, to the rich, who reply, not now, not now, the dog's birthday is passing into history with all its marvelous music!

The Epic

They have lost their baby down a sewer. They might run to the sea where the sewer empties. Or they might wait where they have lost him; perhaps he returns out of the future, having found his manhood under the city.

Surely they risk his having turned to garbage, an orange peel with a bag of chicken guts.

She is not sure she could love an orange peel with a bag of chicken guts.

It's okay, honey, because everything happens under the smile of God.

But why, in heaven's name, is He smiling?

Because He knows the end.

But aren't we still getting there?

Yes; but He's seen it several times.

Seen what several times?

This movie, the one He produced and directed. The one He starred in . . . You know, the one where He plays all the parts in a cast of billions . . . The story of a husband and wife losing their baby down a sewer . . .

Oh that movie; I cried through the whole thing.

The Family Monkey

We bought an electric monkey, experimenting rather recklessly with funds carefully gathered since grandfather's time for the purchase of a steam monkey.

We had either, by this time, the choice of an electric or gas monkey.

The steam monkey is no longer being made, said the monkey merchant.

But the family always planned on a steam monkey.

Well, said the monkey merchant, just as the wind-up monkey gave way to the steam monkey, the steam monkey has given way to the gas and electric monkeys.

Is that like the grandfather clock being replaced by the grandchild clock?

Sort of, said the monkey merchant.

So we bought the electric monkey, and plugged its umbilical cord into the wall.

The smoke coming out of its fur told us something was wrong.

We had electrocuted the family monkey.

The Floor

FOR CHARLES SIMIC

The floor is something we must fight against. Whilst seemingly mere platform for the human stance, it is that place that men fall to.

I am not dizzy. I stand as a tower, a lighthouse; the pale ray of my sentiency flowing from my face.
But should I go dizzy I crash down into the floor; my face into the floor, my attention bleeding into the cracks of the floor.

Dear horizontal place, I do not wish to be a rug. Do not pull at the difficult head, this teetering bulb of dread and dream . . .

Killing the Ape

They were killing the ape with infinite care; not too much or it runs past dying and is born again.

Too little delivers a sick old man covered with fur.

. . . Gently gently out of hell, the ape climbing out of the ape.

The Kingdom

. . . That's funny, my watch is melting on my wrist.
I wonder if it's painful?
I have been living in my mind.

Out in the provinces of my extremities, where any event seems central, a simple folk of fingers, yoked in habits, are beginning to find evidence that nature is at last changing its mind.

Out in the province of my left wrist, my watch is melting — hands reaching out, curl back to their breast of numbers in the sudden heat. An old man's supplication.
Time the bringer, finally ruins everything.

I have been living in my mind. Pain rides in. I no longer care; the king is sick with doubt.

A Love Letter

Dear Miss,

First of all I want to say that I have enjoyed the imaginary possibility, built of course on the fact that such possibility does exist in nature: I have seen the birds and other forms of nonhumanity occur in such postures that must be with men and women . . . I have imagined myself in such postures with you, where flight was discouraged only by the inherent possibility of the firm horizontal . . .

As men give vast lands to little papers with line and color, I have imagined more on the surface of your body, giving all the universe in this model . . .

Yet, I must be curious about your breasts . . . curious . . . *hungry* is the word, to see, to touch, to taste . . . I am curious as to how your hands undress your body.

I am interested in your mind: will you undress in front of me? Will you permit me the unparalleled pleasure of taking your clothes off?

I feel that if I should have my penis in your vagina I should have your love; for you do not receive the wretched hardness of my desire into the sweet body of yourself without that you have not come to love me for reasons, if love has reasons, I cannot tell . . .

Your admirer

The Mental Desert

The mind is mostly desert. The moon is lovely there, and almost turns the sands to water, save for one's natural logic.

At the paper-doll factory we are issued scissors, and warned not to monkey with our wrists.

I am an extremely serious person, needing no lectures on the care and maintenance of my tools.

I let the wrist business go unchallenged. Why should I invite discourse about monkeys with inferiors who, though in executive station, are nevertheless inferiors in the art of the scissors.

One's work involves the folding of paper, snipping here and there, and finally unfolding a self-portrait of insomniacs in a line of beds, each a night, arranged end to end.

Another ingenious design is a traffic of cars joined bumper to bumper, and so on, depending on how many folds one has made.

One dependable old woman with a rather unlovely stare, creates a masturbator pattern: a chain of lonely men holding their penises, ingeniously attached penis by penis; one long spit through all their groins.

There is the morning-bus motif, the public-toilet motif, any number of old favorites . . . Yet, I thought to give the factory a motif closer to the popular taste; and by this means prove myself worthy of executive station. I created a suicide motif: a chain of paper-doll factory workers attached elbow to elbow, cutting their wrists.

An inferior foreman merely said, you are well on your way to the mis-use of your tools, which may well involve your monkey.

. . . My monkey? I screamed.

. . . Of course the mind is a desert; one grows used to the simplicity of thirst.

Movements

In the wheel is the round shape.

The road is calling only that it is open; and you flow naturally into it, closing something behind you as you fall from the foreground.
You fall from a door. You fall down a road.
You can get nothing, can hold nothing; your finger bones fall away like cigarette butts.

But, in the wheel forever, see it, the shape moving through its own shape like a stillness.

. . . Falling through your whole life, you are breaking apart . . .
But in the round shape of the wheel is the idea which is the bone upon which the flesh of the wheel is fixed . . .

Oh My God, I'll Never Get Home

A piece of a man had broken off in a road. He picked it up and put it in his pocket.

As he stooped to pick up another piece he came apart at the waist.

His bottom half was still standing. He walked over on his elbows and grabbed the seat of his pants and said, legs go home.

But as they were going along his head fell off. His head yelled, legs stop.

And then one of his knees came apart. But meanwhile his heart had dropped out of his trunk.

As his head screamed, legs turn around, his tongue fell out.

Oh my God, he thought, I'll never get home.

The Press of Night

At night when the strings are cut; the only string is an electric cord feeding an electric light.

. . . No, there is no other place.

The electric light presses on the window to keep out the night.

Memory is a string caught in some dark place, beyond even memory; a tangled kite string that will not let the kite rise, even as the metamorphic winds of life will not let it fall.

Thus falls the attention into itself; the lens of the attention withdrawing from the distance; lives in the foreground, having broken from extreme depth.

Chair and table become textures. The eyes grown tactile read the room as Braille. The attention flutters like a moth caught in a room; neither through the window nor into the head of the dreaded self . . .

All out there the night . . .

The Turkey Happening

There were feathers growing on his wall. Thickly. And with pink turkey flesh beneath.

The feathers were spreading across the ceiling. And the floor was beginning to protrude in scaly bird toes like the roots of trees.

He could not tell if he had not now become himself feathers and turkey flesh.

He wondered if he was not now feathers and turkey flesh.

Vomit

The house grows sick in its dining room and begins to vomit.

Father cries, the dining room is vomiting.

No wonder, the way you eat, it's enough to make anybody sick, says his wife.

What shall we do? What shall we do? he cries.

Call the Vomit Doctor of course.

Yes, but all he does is vomit, sighs father.

If you were a vomit doctor you'd vomit too.

But isn't there enough vomit? sighs father.

There is never enough vomit.

Do I make everybody that sick, sighs father.

No no, everybody is born sick.

Born sick? cries father.

Of course, haven't you noticed how everybody eventually dies? she says.

Is the dining room dying . . . ?

. . . The way you eat, it's enough to make anyone sick, she screams.

So I do make everybody that sick . . .

Excuse me, I think I'm going to be sick, she says.

Oh where is the Vomit Doctor? At least when he vomits one knows one has it from high authority, screamed father.

When Science is in the Country

When science is in the country a cow meows and the moon jumps from limb to limb through the trees like a silver ape.

The cow bow-wows to hear all voice of itself. The grass sinks back into the earth looking for its mother.

A farmer dreamed he harvested the universe, and had a barn full of stars, and a herd of clouds fenced in the pasture.

The farmer awoke to something screaming in the kitchen, which he identified as the farmerette.

Oh my my, cried the farmer, what is to become of what became?

It's a good piece of bread and a bad farmer man, she cried.

Oh the devil take the monotony of the field, he screamed.

Which grows your eating thing, she wailed.

Which is the hell with me too, he screamed.

And the farmerette? she screamed.

And the farmerette, he howled.

A scientist looked through his magnifying glass in the neighborhood.

IV

from
The Childhood of an Equestrian

1973

The Automobile

A man had just married an automobile.

But I mean to say, said his father, that the automobile is not a person because it is something different.

For instance, compare it to your mother. Do you see how it is different from your mother? Somehow it seems wider, doesn't it? And besides, your mother wears her hair differently.

You ought to try to find something in the world that looks like mother.

I have mother, isn't that enough of a thing that looks like mother? Do I have to gather more mothers?

They are all old ladies who do not in the least excite any wish to procreate, said the son.

But you cannot procreate with an automobile, said father.

The son shows father an ignition key. See, here is a special penis which does with the automobile as the man with the woman; and the automobile gives birth to a place far from this place, dropping its puppy miles as it goes.

Does that make me a grandfather? said father.

That makes you where you are when I am far away, said the son.

Father and mother watch an automobile with a *just married* sign on it growing smaller in a road.

The Childhood of an Equestrian

An equestrian fell from his horse.

A nursemaid moving through the wood espied the equestrian in his corrupted position and cried, what child has fallen from his rocking-horse?

Merely a new technique for dismounting, said the prone equestrian.

The child is wounded more by fear than hurt, said the nursemaid.

The child dismounts and is at rest. But being interfered with grows irritable, cried the equestrian.

The child that falls from his rockinghorse refusing to remount fathers the man with no woman taken in his arms, said the nursemaid, for women are as horses, and it is the rockinghorse that teaches the man the way of love.

I am a man fallen from a horse in the privacy of a wood, save for a strange nursemaid who espied my corruption, taking me for a child, who fallen from a rockinghorse lies down in fear refusing to father the man, who mounts the woman with the rhythm given in the day of his childhood on the imitation horse, when he was in the imitation of the man who incubates in his childhood, said the equestrian.

Let me help you to your manhood, said the nursemaid.

I am already, by the metaphor, the son of the child, if the child father the man, which is involuted nonsense. And take your hands off me, cried the equestrian.

I lift up the child which is wounded more by fear than hurt, said the nursemaid.

You lift up a child which has rotted into its manhood, cried the equestrian.

I lift up as I lift all that fall and are made children by their falling, said the nursemaid.

Go away from me because you are annoying me, screamed the equestrian as he beat the fleeing white shape that seemed like a soft moon entrapped in the branches of the forest.

The Exile

The young prince is placed under a bed.
He wonders if he is an heir, or the residue of the maid's neglect?

Should he sleep? Or should he simply do nothing?

Even so, time empties out of the banishment. The solitude grows weary and decays out of caring, and the kingdom in the distance merges with other distances.

One cannot help wondering if he had not been meant to be someone else.

And now the laughter of women in the hallway. The movement of feet, the rush and the flush of the living.

And he wonders if he is not just some of the darkness that floats in a dark room, that hangs by mirrors and drifts through the spokes of chairs . . .

Time gives the blossom its final ornament . . .

In All the Days of My Childhood

My father by some strange conjunction had mice for sons.

. . . And so it was in all the days of my childhood . . . The winds blew, and then abated, the rains fell, and then climbed slowly back to heaven as vapor.

Day became night as night became day in rhythmic lengthenings and shortenings.
Time of the blossoming, and time of decline.
The sense of permanence broken by sudden change.
The time of change giving way again to a sense of permanence.

In the summer my brothers' tails dragged in the grass. What is more natural than their tails in the grass?
Upon their haunches, front paws feebly paddling air, whiskers twitching, they looked toward father with mindless faith.

In the winter father would pick them up by their tails and put them in cages.

The ping of snow on the windows; bad weather misunderstood . . . Perhaps all things misunderstood?
It was that understanding came to no question.
Without sense of the arbitrary no process of logic was instigated by my brothers. Was this wrong?

Again in the spring we moved out of doors, and again dragged our tails in the grass, looking toward father with mindless faith.

. . . And so it was in all the days of my childhood.

Metals Metals

Out of the golden West, out of the leaden East, into the iron South, and to the silver North . . . Oh metals metals everywhere, forks and knives, belt buckles and hooks . . . When you are beaten you sing. You do not give anyone a chance . . .

You come out of the earth and fly with men. You lodge in men. You hurt them terribly. You tear them. You do not care for anyone.

Oh metals metals, why are you always hanging about? Is it not enough that you hold men's wrists? Is it not enough that we let you in our mouths?

Why is it you will not do anything for yourself? Why is it you always wait for men to show you what to be?

And men love you. Perhaps it is because you soften so often.
You did, it is true, pour into anything men asked you to. It has always proved you to be somewhat softer than you really are.

Oh metals metals, why are you always filling my house?
You are like family, you do not care for anyone.

The Pattern

A woman had given birth to an old man.

He cried to have again been caught in the pattern.
Oh well, he sighed as he took her breast to his mouth.

The woman is happy to have her baby, even if it is old.
Probably it had got mislaid in the baby place, and when they found it and saw that it was a little too ripe, they said, well, it is good enough for this woman who is almost deserving of nothing.

She wonders if she is the only mother with a baby old enough to be her father.

The Death of an Angel

Being witless it said no prayer. Being pure it withered like a flower.

They could not tell its sex. It had neither anal or genital opening.

The autopsy revealed no viscera, neither flesh nor bone. It was stuffed with pages from old Bibles and cotton.

When they opened the skull it played *Tales from the Vienna Woods*; instead of brain they found a vagina and a penis, testicles and an anus, packed in sexual hair.

Ah, that's better! cried one of the doctors.

The Delicate Matter

. . . As to the courting of a fat woman . . . An old man loves a plump piece of fruit now and again, a pear-shaped goody with big plum bosoms.

. . . As to the courting of a fat woman . . . One says, oh my chicken bone!
No no, that will sound like a piece of garbage from the feast.
No no, he will say, oh my skinny thing, I want to bite you!
No no, she will think the old man mocks her heft.
It is best to ignore her bulk.
It is best to think of her as a great sailing ship; and to stand on her and sing some national anthem.
Women are enthralled by patriotism.

Will she say, get off of my body, you cruel thing?
But you are like a huge water vehicle in which I would sail to paradise!

Will she say, if you do not get off of me I shall not let you get on me for love?
I shall say back to her . . . But I cannot think what.
So I shall sing another national anthem.

. . . As to the courting of a fat woman . . . It is a very delicate matter . . .

The Description

In a garden there arose an old man sitting in a chair.

At first, breaking the earth like a leather egg, his bald head. Day by day, gradually the brow and the unblinking eyes pushed out . . . The grey hair, the earth-filled ears, the nose, earth clinging to the hairs in the nose; then the shoulders, the shawl about the shoulders, the back of the chair encrusted with earth and beetles.

In the moonlight an old man half buried in the earth. In the dawn a man sitting in a shallow sea of mist.

When he had risen completely there was green mold on his shoes and fingernails.

One night we saw him yawn. He stood, and walked quietly away.

For some time now his chair has been sinking back into the earth. We wonder if it is not some kind of elevator of the dead.

A Journey Through the Moonlight

In sleep when an old man's body is no longer aware of its boundaries, and lies flattened by gravity like a mere of wax in its bed . . . It drips down to the floor and moves there like a tear down a cheek . . . Under the back door into the silver meadow, like a pool of sperm, frosty under the moon, as if in his first nature, boneless and absurd.

The moon lifts him up into its white field, a cloud shaped like an old man, porous with stars.

He floats through high dark branches, a corpse tangled in a tree on a river.

The Keeping of the Dead

In the cellar the instrument is best hung by its heels like a ham.

As for the mold that forms on the memento, set aside one day each year for mold scraping; call that day the Memorial Mold Scraping Day.

If a dryer lay is sought for the instrument, the attic serves well. However, a shoetree must be pushed down its throat to keep the organ of complaint from curling up; and mothballs in the grey hair, remembering hungry moths; and baited rattraps in the underwear against the sensuality of rats.

Yet, some like to keep the grandmother in the dining room. They fold her away like a tablecloth of ragged lace and gravy stains; they fold her along the natural wrinkles of her face, placing her gently among the napkin rings and serving spoons.

Be prepared to hear her murmur as she worries whether the upstairs window is closed against the rain . . .

Old Folks

There was once an old man and his wife who lived deep in a wood to guard themselves against the hurt of the young, who are of the brutal joy, for they are with nature, and come as does nature. They from the outside, nature from within, to hurt old folks, who must build deep in a wood that place which is defended by its secret.

The old folks also have guns, and have laid traps, and put bags of acid in the trees.

And are we safe? cries the old woman.

It's the flesh that I fear, guard it as one will, still it dies inside of itself, says the old husband.

We are to be gotten to no matter what we do, screams the old wife.

Your screaming doesn't help, screams the old man.

What helps? screams the old wife.

Nothing, save the hope of a life beyond this one, roars the old man.

But all I have is an old brain wrapped in grey hair; how can I know what I need to know? yells the old woman.

Yelling doesn't help, yells the old man.

What helps? roars the old woman.

Nothing, save that which was before us, and shall continue after us; that cosmic Presence which us so made — But not even *It* lifts one star, or changes the order of one day in our behalf — No, we are alone, and there is no help . . . And so we set traps and keep guns, and make ourselves secret, sighed the old man.

But what helps? screams the old woman.
Certainly not you, luxuriating in an old man's logic, hanging to his wits, which he loses in your incessant questions, roared the old man.

The Smell of Hay and Stars

. . . Some policemen who are chickens . . . Let me explain:

One night as a cow sang a love song to a farmer (the moon, of course) the farmer removed his hat from the bone of thought, and thought, my head must seem sister to the moon; and the moon, that satellite of milk which marries the cow to rapture as cows are married to men by way of their milk, that commerce between the species.

Still, the cow's voice is not bad as against an extreme of bad. So that we take the cow's lowing as a pleasant assault upon a modesty fast dissolving in lieu of the love engendered by the lowing.

Soon the farmer was kissing the cud-slick lips of the cow as the cow rolled its tongue about its mouth, bellowing through the farmer's kisses.

So that the police were called to chaperon the farmer and his cow.

You are chickens, you are chickens, cries the farmer.

And so the police ask for the house of the hen, and there take themselves to the monotony of the chicken perch, where it is that their term of earth is spent, their badges tarnishing, their pistols rusting . . .

And in the moonlight the smell of hay and stars . . .

Through Dream and Suppertime
FOR W. C. W.

The man's head is a vehicle . . . No no, let it sleep.

It has hair growing from its trouble. Hair grows out of the idea of death. The head is death with hair upon it. Also it is a vehicle upon which it is itself to ride through dream and suppertime.

Do you see how the china is full of intestinal matter?

Soon, too soon, the soft mouth of the worm is eating the idea of itself . . .

Ape

You haven't finished your ape, said mother to father, who had monkey hair and blood on his whiskers.

I've had enough monkey, cried father.

You didn't eat the hands, and I went to all the trouble to make onion rings for its fingers, said mother.

I'll just nibble on its forehead, and then I've had enough, said father.

I stuffed its nose with garlic, just like you like it, said mother.

Why don't you have the butcher cut these apes up? You lay the whole thing on the table every night; the same fractured skull, the same singed fur; like someone who died horribly. These aren't dinners, these are post-mortem dissections.

Try a piece of its gum, I've stuffed its mouth with bread, said mother.

Ugh, it looks like a mouth full of vomit. How can I bite into its cheek with bread spilling out of its mouth? cried father.

Break one of the ears off, they're so crispy, said mother.

I wish to hell you'd put underpants on these apes; even a jockstrap, screamed father.

Father, how dare you insinuate that I see the ape as anything more than simple meat, screamed mother.

Well, what's with this ribbon tied in a bow on its privates? screamed father.

Are you saying that I am in love with this vicious creature? That I would submit my female opening to this brute? That after we had love on the kitchen floor I would put him in the oven, after breaking his head with a frying pan; and then serve him to my husband, that my husband might eat the evidence of my infidelity . . . ?

I'm just saying that I'm damn sick of ape every night, cried father.

The Father of Toads

A man had just delivered a toad from his wife's armpit. He held it by its legs and spanked it.

Do you love it? said his wife.

It's our child, isn't it?

Does that mean you can't love it? she said.

It's hard enough to love a toad, but when it turns out to be your own son then revulsion is without any tender inhibition, he said.

Do you mean you would not like to call it George Jr.? she said.

But we've already called the other toad that, he said.

Well, perhaps we could call the other one George Sr., she said.

But I am George Sr., he said.

Well, perhaps if you hid in the attic, so that no one needed to call you anything, there would be no difficulty in calling both of them George, she said.

Yes, if no one talks to me, then what need have I for a name? he said.

No, no one will talk to you for the rest of your life. And when we bury you we shall put *Father of Toads* on your tombstone.

The Ox

There was once a woman whose father over the years had become an ox.

She would hear him alone at night lowing in his room.

It was one day when she looked up into his face that she suddenly noticed the ox.

She cried, you're an ox!

And he began to moo with his great pink tongue hanging out of his mouth.

He would stand over his newspaper, turning the pages with his tongue, while he evacuated on the rug.

When this was brought to his attention he would low with sorrow, and slowly climb the stairs to his room, and there spend the night in mournful lowing.

A Performance at Hog Theater

There was once a hog theater where hogs performed as men, had men been hogs.

One hog said, I will be a hog in a field which has found a mouse which is being eaten by the same hog which is in the field and which has found the mouse, which I am performing as my contribution to the performer's art.

Oh let's just be hogs, cried an old hog.

And so the hogs streamed out of the theater crying, only hogs, only hogs . . .

Toward the Writing

If you wish to write something of value you will get yourself a mouse which has died of some dreadful disease.

. . . Lingering long in bed with a brave smile, marred only by its rodent's teeth, which for love you had ceased to see; or seeing, loved the more as a nakedness . . .

You had to say, please do not smile, I bear your death easier than my will to humiliate.

Do not be brave nor give me cheer.

Bury your ugly face in your pillow and weep for yourself. Think of the springtime and of the newly risen; the soft greens of the sexual beckoning . . .

Oh Mimi, weep into your pillow, I cannot bear your face!

Soon then, when grief has turned to art, you take the mouse to the writing table, and dip its rodent's tail into the ink . . .

. . . But you will need many mice and many prayers . . . And still the writing will wait, for the ritual is long . . .

Antimatter

On the other side of a mirror there's an inverse world, where the insane go sane; where bones climb out of the earth and recede to the first slime of love.

And in the evening the sun is just rising.

Lovers cry because they are a day younger, and soon childhood robs them of their pleasure.

In such a world there is much sadness which, of course, is joy . . .

Conjugal

A man is bending his wife. He is bending her around something that she has bent herself around. She is around it, bent as he has bent her.

He is convincing her. It is all so private.

He is bending her around the bedpost. No, he is bending her around the tripod of his camera.

It is as if he teaches her to swim. As if he teaches acrobatics. As if he could form her into something wet that he delivers out of one life into another.

And it is such a private thing the thing they do.

He is forming her into the wallpaper. He is smoothing her down into the flowers there. He is finding her nipples there. And he is kissing her pubis there.

He climbs into the wallpaper among the flowers. And his buttocks move in and out of the wall.

The Dainty One

I had remained in bed longer than it usually takes one's fatigue to drain off.

Very often there is a song one must sing the whole night through; it repeats, and there is no stopping it. One beats it out with one's canine teeth, or one's toes. It is a musical tic.

I have heard it said that it is a message that one dares not hear. In the dark the unconscious is a dangerous thing. I prefer "Melancholy Baby" to what else I might hear. And so I listen all night to "Melancholy Baby," gnashing each syllable with my teeth.

One feels that things are about to change. I have felt this all my life. It is a readiness that robs every act of meaning, making every situation obsolete, putting the present into the past.

A man is a series of objects placed in a box, the sound of a train, the sounds of his own liquids trickling through the intimate brooks of his body, a certain number of bones, tree shadows that fall through the flesh as nerve patterns, or blood vessels; pourings, exchanges, disconnections . . .

Improvisation mounted in a piece of meat, lying abed in the night. "Melancholy Baby" over and over. Slowed. Out of time . . . Each syllable again and again . . .

The Further Adventures of Martha George
FOR ROBERT BLY

There was a woman named Martha George
who had discovered one day that her chest
was a radio. She turned it on with her left
nipple. A voice came out from between her
breasts: We now present the adventures of
      Martha George. As you remember
      in our last episode Martha had
      been fiddling with her breasts —
      We find her now fiddling with
      her breasts. She turns her left
      nipple. She's afraid it might come
      off. But instead, a voice comes out
      from between her breasts: We
            now present the fur-
            ther adventures of
            Martha George . . .

The Toy-Maker

A toy-maker made a toy wife and a toy child. He made a toy house and some toy years.

He made a getting-old toy, and he made a dying toy.

The toy-maker made a toy heaven and a toy god.

But, best of all, he liked making toy shit.

V

from
The Intuitive Journey

1976

The Terrible Angel

In a nursery a mother can't get her baby out of its cradle. The baby, it has turned to wood, it has become part of its own cradle.

The mother, she cries, tilting, one foot raised, as if in flight for the front door, just hearing her husband's car in the driveway; but can't, the carpet holds her . . .

Her husband, he hears her, he wants to rush to her, but can't, the door of the car won't open . . .

The wife, she no longer calls, she has been taken into the carpet, and is part of it; a piece of carpet in the shape of a woman tilted, one foot raised as if to flight.

The husband, he no longer struggles toward his wife. As if he sleeps he has been drawn into the seat of his car; a man sculptured in upholstery.

In the nursery the wooden baby stares with wooden eyes into the last red of the setting sun, even as the darkness that forms in the east begins to join the shadows of the house; the darkness that rises out of the cellar, seeping out from under furniture, oozing from the cracks in the floor . . . The shadow that suddenly collects in the corner of the nursery like the presence of something that was always there . . .

How Things Are Turning Out

FOR MICHAEL CUDDIHY

A man registers some pigeons at a hotel. They fly up to their rooms. He's not sure that his mind doesn't fly with them . . .

He asks the desk clerk if everything seems all right. He would like to know if the smoke coming out of his cigarette is real, or something the management has had painted on the wall?

The desk clerk has turned his back and is sorting the mail.

Sir . . . , says the man.

But the desk clerk continues to arrange the mail.

Sir, would you look this way for a moment?

I can hear you, I'm just sorting the mail.

I wanted you to notice the smoke of my cigarette . . . Since the pigeons flew up to their rooms . . . You never know about the future, I mean how things will finally turn out . . . Please, could you check my smoke . . . ?

When the desk clerk turns his face is covered with hair, like the back of his head; and the front of his body is like the back of his body.

Where is your front?

My twin brother has the fronts; I was born with two backs . . . I always got the spankings . . . But why regret the past?

That's good philosophy . . .

My best subject.

. . . Tell me, is everything turning out all right?

So far so good . . .

Counting Sheep

A scientist has a test tube full of sheep. He wonders if he should try to shrink a pasture for them.

They are like grains of rice.

He wonders if it is possible to shrink something out of existence.

He wonders if the sheep are aware of their tininess, if they have any sense of scale. Perhaps they just think the test tube is a glass barn . . .

He wonders what he should do with them; they certainly have less meat and wool than ordinary sheep. Has he reduced their commercial value?

He wonders if they could be used as a substitute for rice, a sort of woolly rice . . .

He wonders if he just shouldn't rub them into a red paste between his fingers.

He wonders if they're breeding, or if any of them have died.

He puts them under a microscope and falls asleep counting them . . .

The Abyss

A dining room floats out into space . . .

On earth a cook with a large ham turns back. She calls across the abyss to the living room where people are waiting for dinner, sirs and ladies, I can't get the ham into the dining room . . .

Has the Cook suddenly developed a sense of humor?!
. . . I don't think she's so funny.

Sirs and ladies, I can't get the ham into the dining room . . . Shall I try the split pea soup? Maybe I could get some bread in . . . ? I'll try . . .

Just get the food on the table, and stop trying to be funny!
. . . I don't think she's so funny.
No no, I didn't mean she was successful, I meant she was trying to be funny.
Well, that's something, lots of cooks won't even try . . .

Sirs and ladies, I can't even get the bread into the dining room. Perhaps I could slip a few olives in . . . ? I'll try . . .

What in hell is she trying to pull?! — Olives?! — *She'll try to slip a few olives in?!* You'd better just cut the excuses, and get the dinner on the table!

Sirs and ladies, I can't find the dining room; I don't think it's in the house.

. . . Not in the house?! Have you ever heard of anything so silly?
She's certainly not clever, but she is trying, you've got to give her that.
But she wasn't hired to entertain us.
. . . Do you really think she is entertaining?
No no, I didn't mean she was entertaining, but for some odd reason she's trying to be. Perhaps she wants a raise . . . ?
Well, at least that's more than most cooks'll do, they all want raises; but how many of them really try to be entertaining?

Sirs and ladies, what shall I do . . . ?

Try singing; so far your performance is not very good!
. . . Can she sing?
Who knows? She's tried everything else, we might as well hear her sing . . .

The Feet of the Fat Man

The fat man is asked why he's so fat.

He claims to be only as fat as he needs to be; he doesn't think he's overdoing it . . .

How does one measure? Just being fat seems too much. On the other hand, accepting that there are fat people, how can one tell when a fat man is too fat?

Yet, this man is so fat that his head suddenly slips down into his neck. His face looks up out of his neck. He says, what do you think, do you think I'm overdoing it?

Now his shoulders and chest are slipping down into his stomach and hips — oh my God, he's beginning to fold down like porridge into his thighs!

He's definitely too fat, his bones won't support it.

God, he's going into his calves! His ankles are beginning to bulge.

When he finishes he's only a couple of feet all swollen out of shape.

In one of the feet where the ankle should start is his face. He says, what do you think, do you think I'm overdoing it?

We look into the other foot just to make sure he doesn't have another face; and we are pleasantly surprised to see hair, the foot is full of hair; which we take to be the other half of his head, the back half . . .

The Neighborhood Dog

A neighborhood dog is climbing up the side of a house.

I don't like to see that, I don't like to see a dog like that, says someone passing in the neighborhood.

The dog seems to be making for that 2nd story window. Maybe he wants to get his paws on the sill; he may want to hang there and rest; his tongue throbbing from his open mouth.

Yet, in the room attached to that window (the one just mentioned) a woman is looking at a cedar box; this is of course where she keeps her hatchet: in that same box, the one in this room, the one she is looking at.

That person passing in the neighborhood says, that dog is making for that 2nd story window . . . This is a nice neighborhood, that dog is wrong . . .

If the dog gets his paws on the sill of the window, which is attached to the same room where the woman is opening her hatchet box, she may chop at his paws with that same hatchet. She might want to chop at something; it is, after all, getting close to chopping time . . .

Something is dreadful, I feel a sense of dread, says that same person passing in the neighborhood, it's that dog that's not right, not that way . . .

139

In the room attached to the window that the dog has been making for, the woman is beginning to see two white paws on the sill of that same window, which is attached to the same room where that same woman is beginning to see two white paws on the sill of that same window, which looks out over the neighborhood.

She says, it's wrong . . . Something . . . The windowsill . . . Something . . . The windowsill . . .

She wants her hatchet. She thinks she's going to need it now . . .

The person passing in the neighborhood says, something may happen . . . That dog . . . I feel a sense of dread . . .

The woman goes to the hatchet in its box. She wants it. But it's gone bad. It's soft and nasty. It smells dead. She wants to get it out of its box (that same cedar box where she keeps it). But it bends and runs through her fingers . . .

Now the dog is coming down, crouched low to the wall, backwards; leaving a wet streak with its tongue down the side of the house.

And that same person passing in the neighborhood says, that dog is wrong . . . I don't like to see a dog get like that . . .

The Howling

A large woman has killed her parakeet with an ax; went suddenly berserk; blood all over the house, splashed all over the neighborhood, on the roads leading out of town. It is said that parakeet blood was found in several neighboring towns; that it was even splashed several states away!

She was known to love birds; would put food out in the winter for them.

Her neighbors are curious about her, this large woman who lived alone with a parakeet.

She is splattered with blood. She doesn't seem to see all the people who have gathered to watch her being taken out of her house.

The ax comes out in a bloody burlap bag. The body of the parakeet follows on a rubber stretcher.

The large woman does not seem to see the people who have gathered to watch the authorities lead her out of her house; even as the ax comes out in a blood-soaked burlap bag; the body of the parakeet on a rubber stretcher.

Thin sheets of blood run from the upstairs windows down the walls of the house.

Every so often a tide of blood pours down the stairs from the 2nd floor, and gushes through the front door over the porch, down the front walk into the street.

Someone says the cellar is waist-deep in blood.

The large woman, her arms being held, is led out of her house, down the steps of her front porch into the front yard of her house; people have gathered to watch, even as the ax is carried out in a bloody sack of burlap; two men carrying the parakeet out on a rubber stretcher . . .

Suddenly the large woman begins to howl with a sound deep in herself; it grows loud and awful.
The people stand away. The authorities let go of her arms and begin to back away.

Blood oozes up out of the grass, and drops of blood roll down the telephone poles in long red strokes . . .

Mr. & Mrs. Duck Dinner

An old woman with a duck under her arm is let into a house and asked, whom shall I say is calling?

Mr. and Mrs. Duck Dinner.

If you don't mind my asking, which is which?

Pointing to the duck the old woman says, this here's my husband.

A little time passes and the butler reappears, yes, come right in, you're expected, the kitchen's just this way.

In the kitchen there's a huge stove. The butler says, I'm sorry, we don't have a pot big enough for you; so we're using an old cast-iron bathtub. I hope you don't mind? We have a regular duck pot for your husband.

No no, this is fine, I'll make pretend I'm having a bath. — Oh, by the way, do you have enough duck sauce? says the old woman.

Yes, plenty, and the cook's made up a nice stuffing, too.

My husband'll need plucking; I can undress myself, says the old woman.

Fine, that'll be a great help; we'll have the kitchen girl defeather your husband. — By the way, what would you suggest with duck? asks the butler.

Wild rice, but not too wild, we wouldn't want any trouble in the dining room; and perhaps asparagus spears . . . But make sure they're not too sharp, they can be quite dangerous; best to dull them on a grinding wheel before serving . . .

Very good, Madam. — By the way, do you think that having the kitchen girl defeather your husband might be a little awkward, if you know what I mean? She is rather pretty; wouldn't want to start any difficulties between you and your husband, says the butler.

No worry, says the old woman, we're professional duck dinners; if we started fooling around with the kitchen help we'd soon be out of business. — If you don't mind I'd like to get into the oven as soon as possible. I'm not as young as I used to be, not that I'm that old, but it does take me a little longer these days . . .

The Hemorrhoid Epidemic

They kill the man's monkey because they think it has infected the neighborhood with hemorrhoids.

The man thinks the monkey too good to waste, even if there is only enough monkey to make one boot.

And so he has one boot made, and calls this his monkey-boot.

The boot reminds him of his monkey; the fur on it is exactly like the fur on his monkey.

But, why not, he thinks, is it not made from the same monkey whose fur is like the fur on his boot?

But since there is only one boot he decides he'll either have to have one of his legs amputated or have the boot made into a hat.

He decides to have the boot made into a hat because he has only one head and will not have to have one of his heads amputated.

But when the boot has been made into a hat he doesn't know whether to call it his boot-hat or his monkey-hat.

The hat reminds him of a boot he once had.

But why shouldn't it, he thinks, was it not once a boot?

But that boot reminds him of a monkey he once had.

Yet, why should it not, he thinks, was it not made from the same monkey that it reminds him of?

He is puzzled.

Meanwhile, the hemorrhoid epidemic continues to spread . . .

The Gentlemen in the Meadow

Some gentlemen are floating in the meadow over the yellow grass. They seem to hover by those wonderful blue little flowers that grow there by those rocks.

Perhaps they have floated up from that nearby graveyard?

They drift a little when the wind blows.

Butterflies flutter through them . . .

The Marionettes of Distant Masters

A pianist dreams that he's hired by a wrecking company to ruin a piano with his fingers . . .

On the day of the piano wrecking concert, as he's dressing, he notices a butterfly annoying a flower in his window box. He wonders if the police should be called. Then he thinks maybe the butterfly is just a marionette being manipulated by its master from the window above.

Suddenly everything is beautiful. He begins to cry.

Then another butterfly begins to annoy the first butterfly. He again wonders if he shouldn't call the police.

But, perhaps they are marionette-butterflies? He thinks they are, belonging to rival masters seeing whose butterfly can annoy the other's the most.

And this is happening in his window box. The Cosmic Plan: Distant Masters manipulating minor Masters who, in turn, are manipulating tiny butterfly-Masters who, in turn, are manipulating him . . . A universe webbed with strings!

Suddenly it is all so beautiful; the light is strange . . . Something about the light! He begins to cry . . .

The Dog

A dog hangs in a kitchen, his back stuck to the ceiling. An old woman tries to work him loose with the handle of her broom.

The dog struggles, but the more he struggles the deeper he sinks into the ceiling. He growls and snaps. He implores and whines, swallowing and chewing; his tongue curling in and out of his mouth, as though he lapped water . . .

Finally only the dark little dots of his footpads can be seen. They hear him whining inside the ceiling . . .

The dog . . . ? says the old woman.
The dog is ruined, says her husband.
The dog . . . ? says the old woman.
It's the ceiling, says her husband.
The dog . . . ? says the old woman.
It ate the dog, the ceiling ate the dog, says her husband.
The dog . . . ? says the old woman.
. . . The dog, says the old man.

The Old Woman's Breakfast

The old woman at breakfast, she is so weary she hardly tells herself from the porridge she eats.

She can't tell if she spoons the porridge into herself, or herself into the porridge . . .

The walls melt, and her mind seems to float all over the room like a puff of dust slapped out of a pillow.

She falls into the porridge, she becomes part of it.

She is a porridge of melting walls; her bones no longer different than her flesh, her eyes no longer different than her nostrils.

. . . She begins to spill over the edge of the table . . .

The Pilot

Up in a dirty window in a dark room is a star which an old man can see. He looks at it. He can see it. It is the star of the room; an electrical freckle that has fallen out of his head and gotten stuck in the dirt on the window.

He thinks he can steer by that star. He thinks he can use the back of a chair as a ship's wheel to pilot this room through the night.

He says to himself, brave Captain, are you afraid?

Yes, I am afraid; I am not so brave.

Be brave, my Captain.

And all night the old man steers his room through the dark . . .

Grass

The living room is overgrown with grass. It has come up around the furniture. It stretches through the dining room, past the swinging door into the kitchen. It extends for miles and miles into the walls . . .

There's treasure in grass, things dropped or put there; a stick of rust that was once a penknife, a grave marker . . . All hidden in the grass at the scalp of the meadow . . .

In a cellar under the grass an old man sits in a rocking chair, rocking to and fro. In his arms he holds an infant, the infant body of himself. And he rocks to and fro under the grass in the dark . . .

Hands

An old woman buys an ape's hand for supper. It will not be still, it keeps clenching and unclenching its fist. It might want to pinch her too, she thinks.

Be still, you silly thing, while I clean your fingernails. She wants to clean it up and pluck the fur off it to make it ready for the pot.

She doesn't know whether she'll fry it or boil it, or just simply hurt it, stick it with a fork or a hat pin. She'll hurt it if it doesn't be still!

Be still, you silly thing!

Now the ape's hand is pointing with its forefinger to the cupboard.

The cupboard, huh?

And she is trying to see the angle of the forefinger to see where it points. It points high, something at the top of the cupboard.

What's there? She starts to climb the cupboard, using the shelves as a ladder.

What's up here so grand to be pointed at?

The ape's hand has become a fist and is pounding the table.

I'm looking for it! Stop pounding the table, you silly thing!

The ape's fist continues to pound; the room shakes with it.

Please, please, I'll fall, cries the old woman.

At the top of the cupboard she finds an old dried-out hand covered with dust.

Is this what you want?

The ape's hand on the table opens and closes, as if it would grasp what she has found; and then pounds the table as if to say hurry, hurry, bring it down to me!

All right, all right, I'm coming.

Finally she puts the dried-out hand into the ape's hand. The ape's hand lays the dried-out hand on its back, and strokes the insides of the fingers and palm, until the hand begins to be alive. Then the two hands close into a clasped set, the short blunt thumbs twirling at each other . . .

The old woman sits watching the hands, with their short blunt thumbs twirling, late into the night, until she falls asleep in her chair . . .

Dr. Nigel Bruce Watson Counting

Dr. Nigel Bruce Watson sat before a long piece of sunlight on the floor described by a French door as a series of golden oblongs, three wide and six down.

As he worked his ear for wax he discovered that his ear was loose. He absentmindedly tried to press it back, but it was hanging from his head.

It finally dropped on his shoulder. He tried pasting it back with marmalade which he had been eating for breakfast.

Now he had marmalade all over the side of his head; but the ear refused to stay in place. He put the ear in a cigarette box.

He touched his other ear, and it was also loose.

Better not fool with it, he thought.

But he absentmindedly touched it again, and it fell on his shoulder.

He tried pasting it back with marmalade. But this ear, like the first, refused to adhere.

He put the second ear with the first in the cigarette box, and murmured, I can hear perfectly well without those moth wings.

But now he had great patches of marmalade on the sides of his head. He decided to rub marmalade all over his head and face.

We'll just see what Holmes makes of this, he murmured.

And so Dr. Nigel Bruce Watson, eating marmalade for breakfast, and sitting, as stated, before a long piece of sunlight on the floor, thought best, then, to count the oblongs that made up the larger oblong, which the French door had been describing during the marmalade incident . . .

Now Dr. Nigel Bruce Watson, his head covered with marmalade, his ears in a cigarette box, begins to count . . .

The Dog's Dinner

An old woman was just cooking her dog's dinner when she decided to review the general decline of things in her west window.
Yes, there the old sun bleeds and dies of childbirth.
In the east the anemic child rises, stillborn . . .

When she turns back to the pot where she cooks her dog's dinner she discovers that it is her dog that she is cooking for her dog's dinner.
How strange that when cooking a dog's dinner one cooks the very dog for whom the dinner was being cooked . . .

She takes the steaming pot off the stove and puts it on the floor, thinking that the dog will not be having its dinner tonight, thinking that the dog cannot eat itself . . .

She draws a chair to the pot, and sits there soaking her feet, seeing her dog floating at her ankles in the mist that rises from his dinner.

She thinks, if I cooked the dog, how is it I didn't cook myself? . . . Perhaps next time . . . ?

The Canoeing

We went upstairs in a canoe. I kept catching my paddle in the banisters.

We met several salmon passing us, flipping step by step; no doubt to find the remembered bedroom. And they were like the slippered feet of someone falling down the stairs, played backward as in a movie.

And then we were passing over the downstairs closet under the stairs, and could feel the weight of dark overcoats and galoshes in a cave of umbrellas and fedoras; water dripping there, deep in the earth, like an endless meditation . . .

. . . Finally the quiet waters of the upstairs hall. We dip our paddles with gentle care not to injure the quiet dark, and seem to glide for days by family bedrooms under a stillness of trees . . .

The Overlap of Worlds

The furniture is like models of animals. You can see the dining room table as a kind of bull standing with its cows, the chairs. Or the easy chair with its footstool, the cow with its calf . . .

And they live a life, as if a spirit world and this were overlapped, oblivious to the other.

In moonlight these animals soften and resume their lives, browsing the rugs; as we, upstairs, asleep in our dreams, resume our lives; overlapping and oblivious to the other . . .

In the Forest

I was combing some long hair coming out of a tree . . .

I had noticed long hair coming out of a tree, and a comb on the ground by the roots of that same tree.

The hair and the comb seemed to belong together. Not so much that the hair needed combing, but the reassurance of the comb being drawn through it . . .

I stood in the gloom and silence that many forests have in the pages of fiction, combing the thick womanly hair, the mammal-warm hair; even as the evening slowly took the forest into night . . .

The Lighted Window

A lighted window floats through the night like a piece of paper in the wind.

I want to see into it. I want to climb through into its lighted room.

As I reach for it it slips through the trees. As I chase it it rolls and tumbles into the air and skitters on through the night . . .

Bringing a Dead Man Back into Life

The dead man is introduced back into life. They take him to a country fair, to a French restaurant, a round of late night parties . . . He's beginning to smell.

They give him a few days off in bed.

He's taken to a country fair again; a second engagement at the French restaurant; another round of late night parties . . . No response . . . They brush the maggots away . . . That terrible smell! . . . No use . . .

What's wrong with you?

. . . No use . . .

They slap his face. His cheek comes off; bone underneath, jaws and teeth . . .

Another round of late night parties . . . Dropping his fingers . . . An ear falls off . . . Loses a foot in a taxi . . . No use . . . The smell . . . Maggots everywhere!

Another round of late night parties. His head comes off, rolls on the floor. A woman stumbles on it, an eye rolls out. She screams.

No use . . . Under his jacket nothing but maggots and ribs . . . No use . . .

The Mountain Climber

It is only after I reach the top of the mountain that I discover that it is not a mountain, that I have been crawling across the floor of my bedroom all of my life . . .

Unless I can quickly decide what to do next I shall go on wasting my life!

This *is* the top of a mountain. How could it be else? And I am to be careful not to fall. In fact, I am duty bound to take all precaution. The Universe has entrusted me to myself. And I shall not fail that trust . . .

I have been chosen to be me — OVER HOW MANY OTHERS?!

The Universe has created me to be the witness of its awareness. I am the witness, and the awareness of that witness!

Frankly, the Universe's interests and mine coincide . . .

The Universe lifts its head and stares at itself through me . . .

I inherit the Universe! I am the Universe!

I take out my mountain-climbing food, grains and powders, and mix them with water made from mountain snow. And it all blows up into an immense buffet, served by a helium maître d' balloon on inflated silver dishes . . .

The Song of Dr. Brilliantine

An employer carried a breakfast tray to the bedroom of his tired servant, Dr. Brilliantine, who, on hearing the knuckles of his employer, sighed, enter.

His employer came in and said, I do not like you, Dr. Brilliantine, your bedclothes are sour with years of unlaundered sleep.

Similarly, said Dr. Brilliantine, I do not like you for not liking me; but now you probably dislike me even more for my disliking you, and for which I dislike you even more; we shall end up hating each other.

Nevertheless, Dr. Brilliantine, I have brought you a lovely breakfast.

— As a way, no doubt, of getting into Dr. Brilliantine's bedroom to spy on Dr. Brilliantine, to see how Dr. Brilliantine masticates as he sits in his bed; how the headboard of his bed is stained by Dr. Brilliantine's brilliantined hair; how his fingers break the toast to dip up the yolks of his eggs; how Dr. Brilliantine's eyes water with pleasure as he adds bacon and sausage to his overflowing mouth of egg and toast; how he tries to hide his bloated pleasure with a napkin as though wiping his mouth. You are anxious to know the environmental mood of Dr. Brilliantine's bedroom; you would like to smell Dr. Brilliantine's shaving brush; you would like to look into his shaving mirror to see if after all these years that the mirror has held Dr. Brilliantine's face the mirror hasn't accumulated some secrets about Dr. Brilliantine. You would probably like to look from Dr. Brilliantine's window so that you might imagine how Dr. Brilliantine feels when he looks from his tiny servants' quarter window . . . And how, you think, would Dr. Brilliantine think of the moon rising over that

163

hill? And how is it with Dr. Brilliantine when the rain comes against his window in the time of rain? . . .

Enough, enough, cried his employer, it's getting late, and I have to go down and prepare your lunch . . .

The Intuitive Journey

. . . I commit myself to domestic dogs. I desert my car. And in the evening I am found eating basic earth prepared by a five-year-old wife.

Am I a worm? Must I always eat my passage?

Ah, but the farmers know my worth . . . What is *worth*? What are *farmers*? Why do I say *farmers*?

. . . In the night the naked fat woman is not allowed to be naked; is not allowed to be fat; is not allowed in the night . . .

. . . In the night a woman disguised as a river flows beyond her wildest dreams . . .

. . . A clock looks out of the shivering face of the river. It is time to be away. I start toward the clouds that grow solid in the moonlight . . . Behind the solid wax of death a clown wearing diamond cloth floats with turtles . . .

The car won't start. The prosthetic forehead made of lead. They say man existed on earth a hundred years ago. I venture two hundred. The car won't start. The prosthetic forehead made of lead. It is said that today's breakfast was eaten just this morning. The car won't start . . .

. . . At the cetacea quarries they are digging whales out of the mountains . . .

. . . I take to carrying pails of water; known as the bringer of water; one who brings water as though water were light; changing the past by changing the future . . . Columns that walk in the night, the light of searchlights in my pails . . .

The Incredible Accident

He opens his car door and steps into a great throne room with chandeliers and red carpeting.

There a man wearing knee breeches bows and asks, may I take your head, sir?

What is this? cries the man. I get into my car to go someplace, but see that I have already arrived at the throne room of some unknown king.

Would you like a hot bath before tea, says the man in knee breeches, or would you prefer a tonsillectomy?

But how did this castle get into my car? Or did my car just fit itself around the castle? — One of those incredible accidents one reads about . . .

Won't you come in, sir, says the man wearing knee breeches, the master is waiting to announce you to the further master, who is waiting to announce you to the even further master, who is waiting to announce you to the master beyond even that . . . It takes several thousand years for the final master to even begin to hear of you . . . Best to get an early start . . .

Yes, of course — but, what an incredible accident!

VI

from
The Reason Why the Closet-Man
Is Never Sad

1977

All Those Small But Shapely Things

Aunt Hobbling in her kitchen making a small but shapely breakfast turns and smiles in such a way as to make us aware of the constant space that surrounds her, embracing her, among those things of constant use, things that have become a kind of body music, echoed in the natural sounds of the forest, and in the faint thunders of the distant sky.

She thinks of the finery scarred; rough seductions, as though one could collect a wealth made ugly by breaking through locked doors to those small but shapely interiors . . . One's feelings numbed now by that inner awareness of all the outward shows of all those small but shapely mercies . . .

Yet, in the meantime, the dew, like small glass beads, aligns itself with the sun to make those small but shapely pieces in the grass of what we take to be the purity of light . . .
She floats, suddenly enlightened, like a Kleenex in the wind . . .

Meanwhile, we return once more to the kitchen of Aunt Hobbling, where she turns once more, smiling. And we see her among her things, as part of a collage in which the adhesive withers, so that the piece flutters, or shall we say, shivers, in those small but shapely winds that enter open windows with mercurial desire . . .

The Autopsy

In a back room a man is performing an autopsy on an old raincoat.

His wife appears in the doorway with a candle and asks, how does it go?

Not now, not now, I'm just getting to the lining, he murmurs with impatience.

I just wanted to know if you found any blood clots?

Blood clots?!

For my necklace . . .

The Bridge

In his travels he comes to a bridge made entirely of bones. Before crossing he writes a letter to his mother: Dear mother, guess what? the ape accidentally bit off one of his hands while eating a banana. Just now I am at the foot of a bone bridge. I shall be crossing it shortly. I don't know if I shall find hills and valleys made of flesh on the other side, or simply constant night, villages of sleep. The ape is scolding me for not teaching him better. I am letting him wear my pith helmet for consolation. The bridge looks like one of those skeletal reconstructions of a huge dinosaur one sees in a museum. The ape is looking at the stump of his wrist and scolding me again. I offer him another banana and he gets very furious, as though I'd insulted him. Tomorrow we cross the bridge. I'll write to you from the other side if I can; if not, look for a sign . . .

The Ceremony

With ceremonial regret I lowered a seed into the earth as though I laid it to its final rest . . .

If this seed live again then so shall I.

Which, of course, is sheer nonsense placed in the service of a tongue too long in the damp sleep of its mouth.

From a cloud an ancestor looked out at me. And I thought surely a moment had been reached. And I wasn't wrong, a moment had been reached — and then another — minutes, hours — yes, entire time, before and after me, proceeding in orderly fashion, through me and through the trees like sunlight or a fine rain when the air is so lovely . . .

Had I suddenly become filled with God? Or was it a house falling in upon itself in the distance with a small sigh of dusty desperation? A cloud musty with the smell of old coats . . . The sound of distant calliopes! The trumpeting of elephants!

The Cliff

. . . Standing on a cliff overlooking the sea, sea gulls like scraps of paper blowing over the rocks below. A steady northeast wind, at first refreshing, then chilling; storm coming. . . .

An old fisherman wearing rubber boots makes his way along the cliff. He is carrying something on his back; it is supported by a line over his shoulder which he clutches in his hands. It seems to be a large fish.

On closer inspection it turns out to be an old woman, the line coming out of her open mouth. I imagine a fishhook stuck in her throat.

The old fisherman stops and lets the old woman slide off his back to the ground. Storm coming, he says. He nods in the direction of the old woman on the ground, my wife.

Is she dead? I say, trying to sound concerned.

Oh no, just resting; we always take our walk along the cliffs.

He puts his fingers in her mouth and removes the hook from her throat. There ya be, he sighs.

His wife sits up and yawns; she says, looks like a storm coming.

The old fisherman puts the hook in his mouth and swallows it. And now the old woman picks up the line and begins dragging the old man away. His eyes are shut.

I see the old woman struggling with the line over her shoulder, dragging what seems to be a large fish, as she makes her way through a fine rain just beginning to fall.

175

The Closet

Here I am with my mother, hanging under the molt of years, in a garden of umbrellas and rubber boots, together always in the vague perfume of her coat.

See how the fedoras along the shelf are the several skulls of my father, in this catacomb of my family.

The Coincidental Association

Dr. Glowingly turned to Dr. Glisteningly and said, why are you copying everything I do?

But why are you copying everything I do? replied Dr. Glisteningly.

We can't both be copying, cried Dr. Glowingly.

But I deny it! screamed Dr. Glisteningly.

One of us is copying the other, said Dr. Glowingly.

Admittedly, conceded Dr. Glisteningly, the piling up of coincidence is far too great; either we are both being controlled by a third party, which I rather disbelieve, or one of us is being cued by the other.

I believe you are unconsciously imitating me — no more of it! Dr. Glisteningly; I will not have my spontaneity blurred by your constant echo, said Dr. Glowingly.

Why, look at you, wearing the same deerstalker cap as I wear, the same gray spats, cried Dr. Glisteningly.

Well, it's no secret that I admire your taste — why shouldn't I, isn't it in direct imitation of mine? said Dr. Glowingly.

Perhaps we will not prove who is the copycat, but I do think some effort ought to be made to interrupt this mirror effect of our appearances, particularly the calabash pipes, said Dr. Glisteningly.

I have the corrective, said Dr. Glowingly as he pulled a derringer out of his breast pocket . . . Even of course as Dr. Glisteningly was also pulling a derringer out of his breast pocket . . .

The Cottage in the Wood

He has built himself a cottage in a wood, near where the insect rubs its wings in song.

Yet, without measure, or a proper sense of scale, he has made the cottage too small. He realizes this when only his hand will fit through the door.

He tries the stairs to the second floor with his fingers, but his arm wedges in the entrance.

He wonders how he shall cook his dinner. He might get his fingers through the kitchen windows, but even so, the stove's too tiny to cook enough food; the pots are like thimbles and bottle caps.

He must also lie unsheltered in the night even though a tiny bed, with its covers turned down, waits for him in the cottage.

He curls himself around the cottage, listening to the insect that rubs its wings in song . . .

The Damaged Ape

A little piece of the ape's nostril had fallen off; and then we noticed one of its ears was chipped. On closer examination we saw that one of its fingernails was missing.

By this time, of course, we had grown to love the ape, but still we wondered if it shouldn't be sent back for an undamaged one.

The guarantee slip was still tied to one of its ears: This ape is guaranteed in perfect working order on day of purchase.

But then we noticed something else written on the slip: Floor model, demonstration ape, reduced for quick sale.

Ah, so we did get a bargain without even knowing it.

The ape shyly smiles and presents its cheek for a kiss . . .

But later on in the evening a large hole develops in the ape's stomach from what had seemed earlier only a tiny tear. And all evening we watched the ape's insides slowly coming out all over the rug . . .

Erasing Amyloo

A father with a huge eraser erases his daughter. When he finishes there's only a red smudge on the wall.

His wife says, where is Amyloo?

She's a mistake, I erased her.

What about all her lovely things? asks his wife.

I'll erase them too.

All her pretty clothes? . . .

I'll erase her closet, her dresser — shut up about Amyloo! Bring your head over here and I'll erase Amyloo out of it.

The husband rubs his eraser on his wife's forehead, and as she begins to forget she says, hummm, I wonder whatever happened to Amyloo? . . .

Never heard of her, says her husband.

And you, she says, who are you? You're not Amyloo, are you? I don't remember your being Amyloo. Are you my Amyloo, whom I don't remember anymore? . . .

Of course not, Amyloo was a girl. Do I look like a girl?

. . . I don't know, I don't know what anything looks like anymore . . .

The Fight in the Meadow

The curtains part: it is a summer's day. There a cow on a grassy slope watches as a bull charges an old aeroplane in a meadow. The bull is punching holes with its horns in the aeroplane's fabric . . .

Suddenly the aeroplane's engine ignites; the meadow is dark with blue smoke . . .

The aeroplane shifts round and faces the charging bull.

As the bull comes in the propeller takes off the end of its muzzle. The bloody nostrils, a ring through them, are flung to the grass with a shattered blossom of teeth.

The bull, blood oozing from the stump of its face, backs off, and charges again. This time the propeller catches the bull behind its lower jaw and flings the head into a tree.

The headless bull backs off once more, and then charges down again. The propeller beating at the headless bull, cutting the body away in a great halo of blood, until only the back legs are standing. These run wildly away through the meadow in figure eights and zigzags, until at last they find the aeroplane again. And as they come running down the propeller whacks them apart.

The legs, one with the tail still attached to it, the other somehow retaining both rectum and testicles, scamper off in opposite directions.

The aeroplane turns away; the engine stops.

The shadows are suddenly seen in lengthened form.

The watching cow begins to low . . .

An Historical Breakfast

A man is bringing a cup of coffee to his face, tilting it to his mouth. It's historical, he thinks. He scratches his head: another historical event. He really ought to rest, he's making an awful lot of history this morning.

Oh my, now he's buttering toast, another piece of history is being made.

He wonders why it should have fallen on him to be so historical. Others probably just don't have it, he thinks, it is, after all, a talent.

He thinks one of his shoelaces needs tying. Oh well, another important historical event is about to take place. He just can't help it. Perhaps he's taking up too large an area of history? But he has to live, hasn't he? Toast needs buttering and he can't go around with one of his shoelaces needing to be tied, can he?

Certainly it's true, when the 20th century gets written in full it will be mainly about him. That's the way the cookie crumbles — ah, there's a phrase that'll be quoted for centuries to come.

Self-conscious? A little; how can one help it with all those yet-to-be-born eyes of the future watching him?

Uh oh, he feels another historical event coming . . . Ah, there it is, a cup of coffee approaching his face at the end of his arm. If only they could catch it on film, how much it would mean to the future.

Oops, spilled it all over his lap. One of those historical accidents that will influence the next thousand years; unpredictable, and really rather uncomfortable . . . But history is never easy, he thinks . . .

Journey for an Old Fellow

Can the old fellow get out of the kitchen? It is an arduous journey which will take him through those remarkable conversations of the dining room; and through the living room, where murder is so common that to even notice it proves one the amateur . . . Then the hallway and the stairs to the upstairs of dark bedrooms where boats rock at their moorings . . . Out through the walls grown translucent with moonlight, into a marble world of sheep grazing on the hills of the night . . .

The Large Thing

A large thing comes in.

Go out, Large Thing, says someone.

The Large Thing goes out, and comes in again.

Go out, Large Thing, and stay out, says someone.

The Large Thing goes out, and stays out.

Then that same someone who has been ordering the Large Thing out begins to be lonely, and says, come in, Large Thing.

But when the Large Thing is in, that same someone decides it would be better if the Large Thing would go out.

Go out, Large Thing, says this same someone.

The Large Thing goes out.

Oh, why did I say that? says the someone, who begins to be lonely again.

But meanwhile the Large Thing has come back in anyway.

Good, I was just about to call you back, says the same someone to the Large Thing.

The Long Picnic

An official document blows through a forest between the trees over the heads of the picnickers.

It is the end of summer, and there is only the snow to be looked forward to. The photosynthetic world is collapsing.

Those who have been picnicking all summer in the forest see that their food has gone bad. The blackberry jam is tar, the picnic baskets are full of bones wrapped in old newspapers.

A young man turns to his sweetheart. She's an old woman with white hair; her head bobs on her neck.

The picnickers try to catch the document as it flies over their heads. But the wind carries it away.

What is written on it is that *the summer is over . . .*

The Lonely Traveler

He's a lonely traveler, and finds companion in the road; a chance meeting, seeing as how they were both going the same way.

. . . Only, the road had already arrived at its end; like a long snake, its eyes closed in the distance, asleep . . .

Making a Movie

They're making a movie. But they've got it all wrong. The hero is supposed to be standing triumphantly on the deck of a ship, but instead is standing on scaffold about to be hanged.

The heroine is supposed to be embracing the hero on the deck of that same ship, but instead is being strapped down for an electric shock treatment.

Crowds of peasants who long for democracy, and are supposed to be celebrating the death of a tyrant, are, in fact, carrying that same tyrant on their shoulders, declaring him the savior of the people.

The director doesn't know what's gone wrong. The producer is very upset.

The stunt man keeps asking, now? as he flips and falls on his head.

Meanwhile a herd of elephants stampedes through central casting; and fake flood waters are really flooding the set.

The stunt man asks again, now? and again flips and falls on his head.

The director, scratching his head, says, perhaps the electric shock should be changed to insulin . . . ?

Are you sure? asks the producer.

No, but we might just as well try it . . . And, by the way, that stunt man's not very good, is he?

An Old Man's High Note

The ceiling closes heaven like a door. This old man is local to wall and ceiling, the drawn curtains and the fire in his hearth . . .

His son struggles in the dark above the house, like a rubber boot tumbled and driven in a river. The old man wonders if it is not chimney smoke that creates the tortured ghost.

The old man, who is himself dead but for memory of when he lived, sits then remembering when he was not dead in ghost summers fading like old photographs where shadow and light become less different all the time, all the time, until at last they'll not be different . . .

The old man makes a high note with his voice; holds it; thinks he can hold it indefinitely. It is not a sound usual to the range of his voice or desire. It is the sound of a violin string where a bow of seeming infinite length is drawn on it through the hours of the night.

It is not like a scream that would fill the room with red bits of flesh. It is a high-pitched yellow beam, eeeeeeeee, that goes on and on, neither falling nor rising, without use or emotional intent.

And he wonders why he has never done this before . . . Being so near death, or so far from life; being, as it were, without the desire for either life or death; being between, without leaning one way or the other — why had he never found this high-pitched note in himself before, this one which he holds through the night?

His son struggles in the dark above the house like chimney smoke tumbled and driven in the wind . . . Memory, which is clogged with death and illusion, with thousands of leaves which the mind's eye records as areas of summer . . . All this and more, coffee cups and spoons, doors that opened and closed, all the streets and roads that were at last one, roof slope and shadow, the soft coat of twilight over the day . . . And the high note continues, even as the first pale light begins to describe the earth again . . .

Oyster Stuffing

It was the last Thursday of November, and a large turkey had been murdered . . .

They say he was up in bed reading a cookbook just before sleep. They say he had just handled his pocket watch; perhaps to wind it and see the time. There was a feather caught on the winding stem.

On the table next to the bed was an open ink jar with a quill pen stuck in it. The turkey evidently had been marking a recipe in the cookbook for oyster stuffing . . .

His head, still wearing its sleeping cap, was on the pillow. The body had obviously been dragged through the window and across the yard through the snow . . .

The investigation has been postponed because of the holiday; most of the police will be having Thanksgiving dinner with their families . . .

The Parental Decision

A man splits into two who are an old woman and an old man.

They must be his parents. But where is the man? Perhaps he gave his life for them . . .

I ask the old couple if they've seen their son.

The old woman says, we've decided not to have any children.

The Reason Why the Closet-Man Is Never Sad

This is the house of the closet-man. There are no rooms, just hallways and closets.

Things happen in rooms. He does not like things to happen.

. . . Closets, you take things out of closets, you put things into closets, and nothing happens . . .

Why do you have such a strange house?

I am the closet-man, I am either going or coming, and I am never sad.

But why do you have such a strange house?

I am never sad . . .

The Taxi

One night in the dark I phone for a taxi. Immediately a taxi crashes through the wall; never mind that my room is on the third floor, or that the yellow driver is really a cluster of canaries arranged in the shape of a driver, who flutters apart, streaming from the windows of the taxi in yellow fountains . . .

Realizing that I am in the midst of something splendid I reach for the phone and cancel the taxi: All the canaries flow back into the taxi and assemble themselves into a cluster shaped like a man. The taxi backs through the wall, and the wall repairs . . .

But I cannot stop what is happening, I am already reaching for the phone to call a taxi, which is already beginning to crash through the wall with its yellow driver already beginning to flutter apart . . .

The Tearing and Merging of Clouds . . .

. . . So it is given: we follow as through a tunnel down through the trees into the earth, where the dead swim cleansed of the world; innocent in undiscovered desire . . .

Chains of events hold between points, bridges that are not for the traveler, but for the seer, for whom such bridges are unnecessary . . .

The porridge on the table longs for the ceiling, dreaming of new plasticities . . .

The window watches with all its meadows and rivers, its trees leaning in the wind to see more fully . . .

Everything is made of time, and we go out in waves, accumulating around ourselves in halos of dust; the borders bleeding each into the other; the tearing and merging of clouds . . .

Through the Darkness of Sleep

In sleep: softly, softly, angel soldiers mob us with their brutal wings; stepping from the clouds they break through the attic like divers into a sunken ship.

A handful of shingles they hold, leafing through them like the pages of our lives; the book of the roof: here is the legend of the moss and the weather, and here the story of the overturned ship, sunken, barnacled by the markings of birds . . .

. . . We are to be led away, one by one, through the darkness of sleep, through the mica glitter of stars, down the stairways of our beds, into the roots of trees . . . slowly surrendering, tossing and turning through centuries of darkness . . .

The Unscreamed Scream

A woman thinks she must cook her cat today . . .

Suddenly tears, like theater glycerin, seep up out of her ducts and down her cheeks. She thinks of a plague that might overtake the birds, causing all the birds of the world to die . . . They are raked up like leaves . . . In a few weeks humankind forgets that there ever were birds on earth . . .

The sweet hot lachrymal tide once more overflows as she thinks of music being torn and scattered by the wind; musicians overtaken by sudden flood; an earthquake finally destroying the house of music . . .

Clouds, she thinks of clouds, dark like caves; holes where people wander, having lost their minds; there, those who do evil ride bicycles in mockery of those that stumble forward, mindless, like the blind with broken butterfly hands . . .

She thinks she must cook her cat today . . . Set it on fire! Squeeze it in the door! . . . This to keep herself from screaming . . .

VII

from
The Wounded Breakfast

1985

How Things Will Be

FOR JAMES TATE

. . . The kitchen will always be hungry then. The cupboard won't even find a bone.

The bedrooms will lie awake at night, blank-eyed against the whispery shuffle of hallways wandering back and forth, like blind mice looking for their eyes.

History in voluminous skirts waddled by knocking courage off the table.

The singing by the river turns out to be a radio plugged into the mouth of a corpse.

In a nearby field a butterfly is being folded up by a praying mantis into a small bright package.

. . . A tub of arthritic blood: Mother Hubbard kills the Sphinx.

In a dresser drawer a ruined city of hemorrhoids.

This . . . and the moon . . .

The Way Things Are

There was a man who had too many mustaches. It began with the one on his upper lip, which he called his normal one.

He would say, this is my normal mustache.

But then he would take out another mustache and put it over his real mustache, saying, this is my abnormal one.

Then he would take out another mustache and put it over the other two and say, this one's normal.

And then another over the other three, saying, this one's abnormal.

And after several more layers he was asked why he wanted to have so many normal and abnormal mustaches.

He said, it's not that I want to, it's simply the way things are . . .

Then he took all the mustaches off. They like a rest, he murmured.

The first mustache, which we thought was real, was not.

We mentioned to him that we thought his first mustache was real.

He said, it is, all my mustaches are real; it's just that some of them are normal, and some of them are abnormal; it's simply the way things are . . .

200

The Sculptor

FOR DONALD HALL

There is a time when the dead, not yet fully fallen from the bone, are fleshed with a kind of soapy clay. One waits for this certain ripening. It depends upon the soil, the time of year . . .

Best is the digging in the early dawn, the ground wet with dew, the air with mist. A few crows cry then, and the screech of sea gulls. They sense the unearthing. What is work to me is food to them . . .

Unearthed, I cut the rotten clothes from the flesh, careful of the soft tissues, the female breasts, the male genitals, that they are not detached or deformed.

If it's a fat person I dig out handfuls of belly. I finish it by smoothing it, and finally poking a new navel with my finger.

I pinch and squeeze as mood prescribes. If driven I can turn a man into a woman, a woman into a man!

Once I changed a man into a child by removing certain bones. The result was less than life, yet, more than death; it was art . . .

You

Out of nothing there comes a time called childhood, which is simply a path leading through an archway called adolescence. A small town there, past the arch called youth.

Soon, down the road, where one almost misses the life lived beyond the flower, is a small shack labeled, you.

And it is here the future lives in the several postures of arm on windowsill, cheek on this; elbows on knees, face in the hands; sometimes the head thrown back, eyes staring into the ceiling . . . This into nothing down the long day's arc . . .

The Love Affair

One day a man fell in love with himself, and was unable to think of anything else but himself.

Of course he was flattered, no one had ever shown him that much interest . . .

He wanted to know all about himself, his hobbies, his likings in music and sports.

He was jealous he had not known himself as a child. He wanted to know what kind of a boy he had been . . .

When asked if he thought it would lead to marriage, he said that that was his fondest wish, that he longed to have babies with himself . . .

203

The Matter

In it were the things a man kept, otherwise they were not in the box: a toy person with an arm missing; also a leg.

Actually, both arms were missing. And, as one leg was missing, so was the other; even the torso and the head.

But, no matter, because in it was another toy person. This one was also missing an arm and one of its legs.

Actually, it had no arms at all; same with the legs, the torso and head.

But, no matter, the box was full of armless and legless toys without torsos or heads.

But again, no matter, because even the box was missing . . . And then even the man . . .

In the end there was only an arrangement of words; and still, no matter . . .

Sheep

They are in the house. They move like clouds over the floors.
They are in the bedrooms. They return from the cellar. They wander
in the attic like balls of dust.

A man is sitting in the kitchen, his face in his hands. He is crying, his
tears wetting through his fingers.
The sheep baa and to him gather, licking his hands for salt.

A ewe then sweetly offers herself in heat.
He turns her on her back, his face in the wool of her breast . . .

The Wounded Breakfast

A huge shoe mounts up from the horizon, squealing and grinding forward on small wheels, even as a man sitting to breakfast on his veranda is suddenly engulfed in a great shadow, almost the size of the night . . .

He looks up and sees a huge shoe ponderously mounting out of the earth.

Up in the unlaced ankle-part an old woman stands at a helm behind the great tongue curled forward; the thick laces dragging like ships' rope on the ground as the huge thing squeals and grinds forward; children everywhere, they look from the shoelace holes, they crowd about the old woman, even as she pilots this huge shoe over the earth . . .

Soon the huge shoe is descending the opposite horizon, a monstrous snail squealing and grinding into the earth . . .

The man turns to his breakfast again, but sees it's been wounded, the yolk of one of his eggs is bleeding . . .

The Doorway Trap

A man came to a full-length mirror, which he took to be a doorway, and saw another man about to enter out from the other side. And as he tried to avoid the other man the other man tried to avoid him, allowing neither of the men to pass.

The first man said, I'm afraid we've been caught in the doorway trap; just as I think to move to the left you move to your right. *Right* from your point of view is *left* in my point of view; so is *left* from your intimacy *right* in my personalized understanding of the universe. If we would both move to our respective *rights* then we would both be moved to the respective *left* of the other, and thus be able to pass out of the doorway trap. But no, our reflexes are too slow, just as you correct the vector of your advance I am correcting mine; we end up face to face and have to start again . . .

All this because we don't want any contact with the other, which is the secret of our imprisonment. We imprison each other paradoxically by trying to avoid the other. I lunge left, you lunge right, we meet face to face, embarrassed. We try again, trying to outguess the other, and again meet face to face; neither giving way to let the other pass, nor taking a chance and pushing through . . . But no, darting and lunging like a man and his reflection, coordinated in endless coincidence . . .

My Head

This is the street where my head lives, smoking cigarettes. I pass here and see it lying half asleep on a windowsill on my way to school where I study microbiology, which I finally give up because it all seems too small to have very much meaning in a world which I attempt to live in.

Then I begin my studies in advanced physics, which entails trying to understand atoms and subatomic particles. I give this up too when I finally realize that I have entered a world even smaller than microbiology.

I think then that I should become an astronomer and open myself to the largest view, but see only dots, which the professor says any one of which might have taken millions, or perhaps billions, of years to reach only recently evolved optic nerves; and that in fact any star whose light we accept might be long perished, leaving only a long wistful string of light. And I wonder what this has to do with me or the world I attempt to live in. So I give up astronomy.

I come here now, into this street, looking up at my head lying half asleep on a windowsill, smoking cigarettes, blinking, and otherwise totally relaxed in the way men become when they have lost all hope . . .

A Zoography

A man had a herd of miniature elephants. They were like wads of gray bubble gum; their trumpeting like the whistling of teakettles . . .

Also, he had a box of miniature cattle. When they lowed at sunset it was like the mewing of kittens . . .
He liked to stampede them on his bed . . .

In his closet a gigantic moth the size of a dwarf . . .

Of This World

The old man definitely has wings. You see them when the light is right. They are attached to his faded overcoat, which once blue is turning brown.

The wings are so delicate, so transparent, they don't seem the kind of wings an old man would have. One would expect thick, woody feathers.

Yet, still he wants his hot soup, and wants to sit near the fire and rub the hands, grown thick and stiff, of this life together, to feel the blood of this life in them.

When he takes off his overcoat to sit by the fire I look to see if the wings are still attached to it. And of course they're not. Now the wings are attached to the old sweater he wears. When the fire blazes up the wings are suddenly there. They droop from his sweater and hang down from his chair, the ends lightly crumpled on the floor.

He rubs his hands together gazing into the fire. How he enjoys the fire of this world . . .

The Paddlers' Song

. . . Paddling for twenty years against the current. We haven't moved. If anything, we've lost.

But the river closes the wounds of our displacements with neither scar nor pit.

The shore was always there. We could have tied our boat and come as far.

We might even have landed and put leaves together and had a roof, and watched the river with a pleasure grown aesthetic; the river that closes the wounds of our displacements with neither scar nor pit.

We might have traveled inland to great cities to sit in drawing rooms; and against the mild baritone of cellos heard clever persons so describe the human condition as a place on a river, where men drown in the soft sounds of rushing water; the river that closes the wounds of our displacements with neither scar nor pit.

We might even have flown (in the Twentieth Century men flew), to see the river of our struggle as one more thread from the great head of oceans . . . River that closes the wounds of our displacements with neither scar nor pit . . .

Charity

An old woman was burying a dead mop . . .

You were a good mop, but you died. And now I have only a broom, my false teeth, a couple of bunions and, if the sun shines, a shadow. All else have died . . .

But then she discovered that her mop was not dead, just unconscious. Smelling salts, and her mop was as good as ever . . .

Meanwhile, she had developed a toothache in one of her false teeth.

Ow ow, she cried, pain is too painful. She wished her false teeth would die.

Suddenly her shadow went into an epileptic fit . . .

My God, she cried, nothing keeps.

And again her mop fainted.

Her bunions began to sing hymns in her shoes.

Her knees began to accuse each other of having switched places . . .

And at last only her broom remained true to the idea of charity . . .

The Human Condition

Can we depend on human intelligence to save itself? said Dr. Gas as he began pushing the horns of his mustache into his nostrils.

From what, Dr. Gas?

From itself, said Dr. Gas as he blew his mustache out into a handkerchief.

But, Dr. Gas, how can an intelligence, not intelligent enough not to be a danger to itself, be intelligent enough to save itself?

Simply by stopping being so darn silly; human intelligence is just too darn silly, said Dr. Gas as he began once more stuffing his mustache into his nose.

But, Dr. Gas, how do you see the human intelligence as dangerous to itself?

By being so darn silly, said Dr. Gas as he once more blew his mustache into his handkerchief.

And as Dr. Gas started to comment further on the condition of the human condition he was interrupted by someone saying, no matter, Dr. Gas, your mustache trick is just too silly, even as Dr. Gas was again pushing the cusps of his mustache into his nose . . .

The Father Who Bowed

A father presented himself. He said, ladies and gentlemen, your father . . .

His family applauded.

He bowed . . .

Ladies and gentlemen, he began, it has come to my attention over the last few decades that we are run up against a biological barrier . . .

His family began to applaud . . .

No, he began again, do not say that age is beauty, that the white-haired old woman trying to see the sock she darns through cataracts is worth the droppings of a rat.

No, I should say more service to the healthy microbe in the rat's droppings than the poor darning that comes of arthritic hands and eyes in cataract . . .

No, indeed, more to be said for lesser forms than men astride their graves!

. . . We weary the promise unfulfilled, the downward repetition that ends in utter, utter death . . .

His family applauded . . .

Ladies and gentlemen, he began again, let us end this terrible business: stuffing brother George into the toilet like a turd; Mother into the garden like a potato; sister Ann up under the roof like an old cobweb; for me, the garbage can . . .

His family began to cheer; they were on their feet crying, bravo bravo, encore encore.

You do me too much honor, he sighed as he bowed; the curtain slowly coming down . . .

Darwin Descending

Do you believe in evolution, oh, thing of easy answers?
Do you believe Darwin was descended from a thing more jaw than head?

. . . Imagine an early Darwin roving the trees, nostalgic for the future . . .
A female Darwin slaps him on the back of his small, but promising head; whatcha thinking about, ya brainless brute? she peeps.
I was just wondering about the origin of species, he twitters.
You haven't the brains of a modern chimpanzee, she screeches.
Yeah, but I think that's where I'm evolving; a large-brained primate with an opposable thumb, with which I shall oppose all of nature, twitters Darwin.
Oh, stop it, you're hardly on to tools; why, you haven't even fooled with fire yet, she hoots.
Yeah, but one day, Darwinette, I'm gonna talk good, and even learn how to write *talking* with a fountain pen . . .
Promises, promises . . .

But, as we all know, Darwin did descend.
It was at a cocktail party, and he had been roving the upstairs halls looking for the indoor plumbing.
And now he was returning via the carpeted stairway.
Everyone turned and applauded: look, the descent of Darwin!

On the Eating of Mice

A woman was roasting a mouse for her husband's dinner; then to serve it with a blueberry in its mouth.

At table he uses a dentist's pick and a surgeon's scalpel, bending over the tiny roastling with a jeweler's loupe . . .

Twenty years of this: curried mouse; garlic and butter mouse; mouse sautéed in its own fur; Salisbury mouse; mouse-in-the-trap, baked in the very trap that killed it; mouse tartare; mouse poached in menstrual blood at the full of the moon . . .

Twenty years of this, eating their way through the mice . . . And yet, not to forget, each night one less vermin in the world . . .

The Head Bumping in the Dark

My parents always kept an old man in the rafters of the house. It brings good luck that an old man is perched in the dark against the roof.

If you can hear his bald head bumping the roof as he shifts in the dark you may have one wish . . .

Now it was that I had married a wedding cake. And it was that we took luck to live in the rafters of our house, and listened for his bald head against the roof to begin our conjugal delights . . .

I took my bowl of oatmeal to the bedroom. I put my chicken salad on the bed. I said to my barrel of beer, did you ever see a man in full extension?

My bag of feathers giggled.

Did you ever see a long thing like this? I said to my pot of cornmeal.

My peach tree sighed as if the wind were breathing through her peaches. And we heard the old man's head bumping in the dark against the roof . . .

The Rat's Legs

I met a rat under a bridge. And we sat there in the mud discussing the rat's loveliness.

I asked, what is it about you that has caused men to write odes?

My legs, said the rat, for it has always been that men have liked to run their hands up my legs to my secret parts; it's nature . . .

The Dark Side of the Moon

When a man returned he saw that everything had been melted, puddled flat. His fedora looked like a large rare coin. The dead moth on the windowsill looked like a brown cloth draped from the windowsill. The lamp on the night table looked like a fried egg . . .

He went to ask his landlady about all this melting, but found that even she was melted; on the floor like a wall-to-wall picture of the moon; one breast the Sea of Tranquillity, one eye the Sea of Opticus . . .

He looked for the vulva, and not finding it, decided it must be on the dark side of the moon . . .

Good Son Jim

Poor people who do not have the price of a fence ask son Jim to be a fence for the chicken yard, that is, until their ship comes in; which no one believes because they live inland.

But what's the good of a fence around a chicken yard where there ain't no chickens?

Did you eat them chickens, Jim?

No, we ain't never had no chickens.

Then what are you doing fencing what we ain't got?

I don't know, I forget . . .

Maybe you better be a chicken. But don't wander away, because we ain't got a fence to keep that stupid bird from wandering into the neighbor's yard and getting itself killed for Sunday dinner, said his father.

Heck, I'll just peck around the house; lots of tasty worms under the porch, said son Jim . . .

How It All Gets Kind of Fluttery

An animal named Archibald was just hanging his pet overcoat in the hallway closet, using his teeth, when a large biped picked Archibald up by Archibald's tail and said, Archibald, dearest, how would you like a nice sock in the eye, or a star-studded punch in the snoot?

Actually, Archibald doesn't think he'd like either; anyway, Archibald has to ask his pet overcoat some questions.

Oh, the heck with that overcoat, said the biped, I want to bop you around a little.

Archibald doesn't like being held by his tail because it makes him feel oh, so . . . so avuncular.

Oh, don't be so grouchy, said the biped, you'll get lipstick on my collar.

No no no! Archibald doesn't want any more fuss made about his good looks.

Say, let's play you're an ape and I've just joined the navy and we're having a scrap over a box of chocolates, said the biped.

Will you let go of my tail, you're making me feel oh, so . . . so avuncular; besides, my pet overcoat doesn't like to see me upside down — whoops! cried Archibald.

Whoops! cried the biped.

Let go of my tail, you fart, the train doesn't stop here anymore; next town over, yowled Archibald.

. . . You know, said the biped, you're beginning to interest me, something about you that's different . . .

I know, said Archibald, and that's how it all gets kind of fluttery . . .

I love you, too, said the biped . . .

The Philosophers

I think, therefore I am, said a man whose mother quickly hit him on the head, saying, I hit my son on his head, therefore I am.

No no, you've got it all wrong, cried the man.

So she hit him on the head again and cried, therefore I am.

You're not, not that way; you're supposed to think, not hit, cried the man.

. . . I think, therefore I am, said the man.

I hit, therefore we both are, the hitter and the one who gets hit, said the man's mother.

But at this point the man had ceased to be; unconscious he could not think. But his mother could. So she thought, I am, and so is my unconscious son, even if he doesn't know it . . .

223

Pigeons

If a scientist had bred pigeons the size of horses, they had great masterly breasts with pink pigeon nipples; and they strutted, and cooed with voices as deep as bulls' . . .

They were soft, like stuffed furniture designed for huge cripples.
And the scientist would have to think about cutting them open to make sure there wasn't money hidden in their stuffings . . .

And they would be like the terrible mother when they tilted their heads, staring one-eyed; their great masterly breasts, so soft; their pink pigeon nipples . . .

And the scientist would really have to think about cutting them open to see if Benjamin Franklin's kites weren't trembling in the thunderstorms of their breasts . . .

The Rat's Tight Schedule

A man stumbled on some rat droppings.

Hey, who put those there? That's dangerous, he said.

His wife said, those are pieces of a rat.

Well, he's coming apart, he's all over the floor, said the husband.

He can't help it; you don't think he wants to drop pieces of himself all over the floor, do you? said the wife.

But I could have flipped and fallen through the floor, said the husband.

Well, he's been thinking of turning into a marsupial, so try to have a little patience; I'm sure if you were thinking of turning into a marsupial he'd be patient with you. But, on the other hand, don't embarrass him if he decides to remain placental, he's on a very tight schedule, said the wife.

A marsupial? A wonderful choice! cried the husband . . .

With Sincerest Regrets

FOR CHARLES SIMIC

Like a monstrous snail a toilet slides into a living room on a track of wet, demanding to be loved.

It is impossible, and we tender our sincerest regrets. In the book of the heart there is no mention made of plumbing.

And though we have spent our intimacy many times with you, you belong to an unfortunate reference, which we would rather not embrace . . .

The toilet slides away on another track of wet . . .

The Thickening

A cook sleeps. On her lap a bowl of thickened material; a wooden spoon standing in it.

As she sleeps she absentmindedly pokes her head with the wooden spoon, and has flecks of the thickened material dotted in her hair. She sighs and snores . . .

Her mistress says, cook, you're not doing work.

The cook nods and yawns.

But, cook, you have thickened material dotted in your hair.

Oh, ma'am, is you drowsy, too?

No no, I'm too excited — it's stuff from your mixing bowl. What is that stuff that's so wondrously thick in your mixing bowl?

I don't know, ma'am, some kind of stuff what's got thick . . .

It certainly looks thick, and you've got it dotted in your hair . . . Will you dot it in my hair? — I command it!

Then the master comes to see the thickened material, and wants it dotted in his hair; wonders what it would feel like dotted in groin hair . . .

No no, cries the mistress, you cannot show cook your penis.

Of course not, cries the master, what do you take me for, someone who shows his armpits to cooking women? Frankly, my secondary hair is none of her business . . . Mind your own business, cook, or I shall really have to take measures!

But the cook has fallen back asleep, and the thickened material has grown even thicker, as has the dark of the deepening dusk . . .

The Tunnel

I went tunneling into the earth . . .

My wife and I, going through an inventory of reasons, found nothing sufficient to the labor.

Still, she allowed, as I, that a direction once started, as if desire, and the desire to be desired, were mutually igniting, drew the traveler to its end without explainable reason . . .

Yet, does not the southern direction in extreme horizon look to the north, even as that of the north, finding the apex of its final arc, nod wearily south . . . ?

So I went tunneling into the earth, through darkness that penetration only makes darker, faithful to the idea of light, said always to be at the end of tunnels; perhaps not yet lit, but in the universe moving in rendezvous, thus to shimmer under the last shovelful of earth . . .

The Wheelbarrow

Cows they had, many, drifting like heavy clouds in the meadow.

But it was a wheelbarrow they didn't have. They studied catalogs and prayed.

At last despairing the future they tied wheels to the front legs of a cow; two stout men lift the hind legs and wheel the cow about the farm.

The other cows, having never seen a wheelbarrow, turn and look. Then, turning again, they drift out like clouds into the meadow . . .